ABOUT ME

I grew up in a household of faith, my parents are Pastor and First Lady. With saying that, God through them has brought me to an understanding that there is a God, but very specifically *one God, Jesus the Messiah*. I wasn't always a believer, nor was I ever perfect. As a pastor's kid you can feel pressured to believe in God, but I never felt that. My parents showed me the evidence of Christ and I heard His gospel. At a young age I was already called to ministry and for that I was attacked heavily by those my age. I was picked on, mentally abused, had so many trust issues, anxiety, but God. God was my cure, my medicine if you will, that I took not only to cope, but to get *over* what was done to me. Prior to this I was molested by an older friend, with that came confusion, anger, bitterness, trust issues(*as I've stated before*), fear, homosexuality, pornography, and lust. God is a Deliverer and a mighty Healer, I've come in the name of the Lord to declare both that Father and the Son that by His Spirit you may know *Him*. Praise God! *Lord, I know that you will get the glory out of this one!*

Foreword

1 Corinthians 3:2 states, *"For other foundation can no man lay that is laid, which is Jesus Christ."* From this scripture we shall be truly dissect the Bible, we shall break down the hidden things that the counsel of God has unleashed upon the earth. We shall point out things that you may not like necessarily, but in the end I pray for an eternal understanding and knowledge of the God in heaven. I pray that God through this book helps you to understand what He knows as His people. Many have found things that God has not given, they aren't even found *in the Word of God, there is no scriptural basis to their findings(begin with the Word and end with the Word of God).* The Bible says to *test every spirit according to their fruit, and if their fruit does not equate to their doctrine or doings then they aren't of what they speak. Remember friends, that as the wise God had stated in the day of reckoning, "A good tree cannot bring forth bad*

fruit, and a bad tree cannot bring forth good fruit." Matthew 7:18, KJV.
So, test the fruit that I bare friends, and if the Word of God, if the Spirit of God has no place in me, I shall die a part from the Lord Jesus Christ, and not be resurrected in the Life that He promised. However, if my fruit are correct and good, I shall branch out by the Spirit of God, and by the grace of Jesus Christ. And to live accordingly in this life and the next, reigning with Christ in the heavens. Praise God for this book, for it has blessed me, and I believe that the God of heaven and the earth shall bless you with this gift from heaven, Amen. Selah.

———

1. *Foundation*

God created the heavens and the earth, every walking and breathing creature, every flower, tree, lastly and most importantly He created us. First, Adam, the "father of humanity", secondly, Eve his wife the "mother of humanity". He created us fearfully and wonderfully (Psalm

139:14) in His Wonderful image, giving us the ability to think, feel, free will, gave us a world, and a land to rule over in obedience to Him. We were perfect in every way at the beginning, but when Adam ate of the forbidden fruit we fell into what Satan had against God's creation, his own sin, carnality. This gave him dominion over what God, the King of all things, gave us.

What are we to do? We were once perfect! We were made in the image of God, our Creator there wasn't even a blemish of sin, or a thought that was evil. Now, with saying that we cannot just blame Satan for Adam and Eve's sin, he spoke lies, *but* both Eve and Adam put aside the commandment of the Lord. In which He said, *"You may eat of any fruit from any tree in the garden, but not the tree of knowledge of good and evil. For when you do you shall surely die."(Genesis 2:16-17, KJV.)*

God warned, but we all know that the King has foreknowledge, as in He knows all things before they happen. So you may be asking, 'Why didn't He just stop them?' Don't forget, God gave us free will friends this land was ours to have dominion over yet still to yield and be subject to the LORD in obedience. Because they didn't heed to His Words and listened rather to the destroyer, so, we fell into sin.

What is sin? What is the essence of it? Let me tell you, it is the willingness to reject and do the opposite of the will of God. Separation from the Creator. Have you ever heard the Bible talking about the enmity? This helps with, what the essence of it is. In Genesis 3:15, we see that the Lord puts an enmity against the serpent and the woman. The root word for enmity is "enemy", deriving from the Greek word also used in the New Testament as enemy(Scofield Study Bible commentary, KJV). Sin is the enmity against God, because we are now in sin, the way we think, our nature, has been tainted by it, it is an enmity against God. Our thought process is also in the New Testament known as carnal, living in carnality, this adds to the essence of what sin is and what it produces. Separation from God, comes because Satan's spirit has entered corrupting our nature, but the way to redemption and salvation is only by following God and His Way through His Son, Christ Jesus.

Why is following God's will and being obedient to Him *so* important? Why do we have to follow His Way to receive life? Why is

He the only way to it? We must understand that if we look at the beginning of Genesis, that *Christ* is the God of Life, that He is life itself giving it to whom He desires and according to His Divine will.(*see John 11:25: Jesus saith unto her, I AM the resurrection, and the life: he that believeth in Me, though he were dead, yet he shall live.*) His Way has proven to bring forth life, note the fall of Adam and Eve and their willingness to oppose the will of God, this brought death upon them just as God warned. This death that God speaks of isn't just a natural death, Adam and Eve were to be immortal, perfect, and without blemish unto the Lord living in the presence of His Spirit, they themselves were *"living spirits"* alive to the fact and realization of our God, that is not separated from Him, no barriers nor any kind of wall between them and the Savior. Once they stepped out of the will of the King, they fell from their spirituality(rather taking upon *flesh or the enmity, carnality see Romans 8:1-8)*, losing their direct access to the Most High, receiving the spirit of death(Satan) in and around them. We clearly see that following the way of sin, leads to death(Romans 6:23)both physically and spiritually(also see in Revelation, the *second death)*.

Choosing to follow the way of God, for me personally I'd have to say has been one of the best decisions I could have ever made in my *entire life.* My God has been exactly Who He said that He was: a Provider, a Wonderful Counsellor, the Everlasting God, and the Prince of Peace(Isaiah 9:6). Christ found me and I found Him by the Grace of His Father, whom He was sent by to restore humanity and to bring us back to His likeness and stature.(Reread, the previous line again, and compare it with the first part of God's own likeness in Genesis.) This brings me to my next point: *Who exactly is Christ? Is He separate from the Father? Is He separate from the Spirit of God(the Holy Ghost)? Is He One with the Father in heaven?*

There are different beliefs that claim the Father, the Son, and the Holy Spirit are three divine yet distinct beings and yet in one unity, this is the *trinitarian* view of the God. Another view states that the Father and the Son rule *side by side and are distinct beings,* but the Spirit of God is God Himself. Lastly there is *monotheism*, which is the belief in the One True God dwelling in fullness in Christ. Let's compare the scriptures with each belief system starting with the trinitarian view.

The trinitarian view is considered rich in it's idea, but is it truly considered rich and holy according to the scriptures? As I stated before that this view declares that the Godhead is divided into three distinct Divine beings, yet being in one unity with one another. They declare that by God saying, "*Let us create man in our image, after our own likeness*," (Genesis 1:26) that it clarifies and points to the holy trinity that they were all there at the time of creation. They also ask about how could Jesus be the Holy Ghost when Jesus said that we could deny Him, but not the Holy Ghost. Also, they point out when in God's Word says, "For God so loved the world, that *He sent His Only begotten Son*." But we must search the scriptures, and as the word declares study to show yourself approved, and when you read, read to get an understanding(or *in all thy getting, get an understanding, Proverbs 4:7, KJV)*. We must not look with our carnal eye of the enmity, but with the eyes of the Spirit of the Lord God that when He says, "For whosoever speaketh a word against the Son of Man it shall be forgiven of him, but whosoever shall deny the Holy Ghost it shall not be forgiven of him." (*Matthew 12:31-32*)Why does He says this? How can He say this if He is the Holy Ghost? Well let's break it down, *for ye shall blaspheme the Son of Man*, we must remember that the scriptures testify that God came in the form of a man, a bondservant, or as the Bible says and I quote "a little lower than angels" yet and was still God. We know that the Holy Ghost represents the power of God. So with saying that we can conclude by scriptural evidence, understanding that God is His Spirit and the Son of God is the Father, this is what He says so that you may understand, "You can deny the person of the Son of Man in His appearance, the servant of God, but you cannot deny and blaspheme the power that I do it by, the Holy Ghost(or My Spirit)." He was quick to rebuke, or correct the Pharisees when they said that Jesus casted out by the prince of demons and not by God(or Himself), that's blasphemous and denying the power thereof in Christ the Godhead, the Head of all principality.(They were blinded by the reputation of Jesus, and their own jealousy that their hearts weren't able to be opened to receive the True knowledge of Who He was and is.

Amen.) Amen there are so many scriptures that disproves this view in its entirety. One that clearly, and utterly destroys this philosophy is Colossians 2:8-10,

⁸ Beware lest any man spoil you through philosophy and vain deceit, after the tradition of men, after the rudiments of the world, and not after Christ.

⁹ For in him dwelleth all the fulness of the Godhead bodily.

¹⁰ And ye are complete in him, which is the head of all <u>principality</u> and <u>power.</u>

¹¹ In whom also ye are circumcised with the circumcision made without hands, in putting off the body of the sins of the flesh by the circumcision of Christ:

¹² Buried with him in baptism, wherein also ye are risen with him through the faith of the operation of God, who hath raised him from the dead.

Let's look at another scripture, Isaiah, *⁶ Unto us a child is born, unto us a Son is given: and the government shall be upon his shoulder: and His Name(or titles) shall be called Wonderful, Counsellor, The mighty God, The everlasting Father, The Prince of Peace.*

⁷ Of the increase of His government and peace there shall be no end, upon the throne of David, and upon His Kingdom, to order it, and to establish it with judgement and with justice from henceforth even for ever. The zeal of the LORD of Hosts will perform this.

So we see clearly that the idea the thought of God when it pertains to Him and His Word is that He is Divinely One Being, not three. In essence and in the way He moves and the power of His might and genius *may* be seen as *three persons*. If you look with the Spirit of God, reread Isaiah 9:6 and only by the Spirit of God can I tell you what it clearly states: *For unto us a (singular)child is born, unto us a Son(one person or in this case Deity, and we know from scripture that God declares to be One God, and that He is the only God that exists) is given: and the government shall be upon His shoulder: and His Title(s) shall be, Wonderful, The Holy Spirit, God the Father, and the Son. (Whose Name is later to be revealed as Jesus the Christ.)*

Going back to *Colossians 2:8-12*, we as His servants by His Spirit should be able to understand exactly what these two scriptures entail is that Christ is and was Emmanuel as it says in *Matthew 1:24*, which means "*God with us.*" That He has all the fullness of the Godhead within Him and we are complete in the One True God that ascended and descended being lifted up to the Highest to fill all things(with His Spirit) Ephesians 4:7-13. Those that believe that Christ the Son, the Father, and the Holy Ghost are *different persons*, different deities as we look at the scriptures are enemies to the faith, or members of Apostasy, rejecting the Deity of Christ, and the fullness of Him, and equally one not just in unity but in stature, in spirit, and person with the Father and the Holy Ghost.

Some of you that read this will reject what I have written, but since you have read it you are now held accountable of the Truth and what it entails and we can also include with all confidence, with confirmation by the word of God, "*that you are following the traditions of men, and the rudiments of this world, and not after Christ, the Godhead.*"

There are so many other scriptures that I could use to clarify my statements, but the list is long, for if you allow the Spirit of God to teach you on this matter you will find scriptures about the Oneness of God throughout the entire Bible. Here is another as if you struggle from a trinitarian view, John 14:6-9,20, Genesis 1:26-27, 1 John 5:5-12, Isaiah 40: 3-5 and please reread the scriptures I have given you by the Spirit of God and study them. Study to show yourself approved my friends and if your doctrine stands why are so many scriptures, which has been proved for reproach and doesn't have a flaw in it can come against it? Why doesn't it support it? You have to remember Satan is cunning and crafty, listen not to the traditions of men and rather to what the Spirit of God has to say. *Be no longer tossed to and fro by every wind of every doctrine be made whole in the One Who created you and that is Christ(Ephesians 4:14).* Be not afraid to step out and be different from those that believe this for when they hear of this from you they will reject it with anger and indignation, but let that not stop you for I say unto your that they will receive their reward, if they do not come to the truth when it has been so clearly presented to them through you by the Spirit of the Most High.

For they shall say you speak blasphemous words against the holy trinity, but is it holy and rich when heaven and God's Word doesn't support it? They shut up heaven for you to not receive knowledge and become greater than them, but they do not try to even reach heaven themselves nor do they study to show themselves approved. The only time they read their Bibles is when they are preparing to preach other than that they don't consult the Spirit of God for what they speak, but go by their own conscience and what makes sense to them. Pray and constantly keep them in your prayers for they follow the laws and rule of men rather than the law of God, being legalistic and systemic in all their ways, and prohibits the flow and of the anointing of the Holy Spirit. For those that don't follow Christ their end result isn't what they expect it to be. Amen, all Glory belongs to the Father in Heaven by Him that Rose from the grave, Christ Jesus His Servant.

On to the second belief that Christ and the Father are separated beings ruling side by side. Is it rich in value if the word of God doesn't support it? Is it to be held onto as a belief or is it a tradition created by men alone? Let's compare it with scripture.

Starting out we can first look at the very popular scripture that states that Jesus went to sit on the *right hand* of God. With the carnal mind there is no way that we can understand at all what those *highly* significant words mean to us as believers in Christ. This belief also may entail the absence of the Holy Ghost and the evidence of speaking in tongues(*Acts 2:3-5*). I have a few questions I need to ask you my brothers and sisters in Christ that if Christ is to be glorified, magnified to the highest, you pray in His Name, make it all about Him where does God the Father of heaven go? Does He fade to the background no longer with power or purpose? See the words of Jesus the Christ, the Son of the Living God my friends, " All *authority*(or *power*) has been given to *Me in heaven and in earth*. Go ye therefore, and teach all nations, baptizing in the *Name* of the Father, and of the Son, and of the Holy Ghost: Teaching them to observe all things whatsoever *I have commanded* you and, lo, *I am* with you alway, even unto the end of the world." **Amen**. (*Matthew 28:18-20*)

So does the God of the Old Testament Who divided the Red Sea, who turn the rivers into blood, the One who created the heavens and the earth give up His power? Does He retire giving all things to another God? Isn't He a Jealous God? Didn't He say that He wouldn't share his glory with anyone? We must search the scriptures to see if He has mentioned and declared these things. The book of Isaiah is wonderfully and powerfully written by the prophet interwoven with the mysteries of God, and His Servant, the Messiah written by the influence of the Holy Ghost of God.

God clarifies many things and states many warnings concerning His Servant whom He had sent and His Deity. Let's start with Isaiah 40:3-5(KJV), *³ The voice of him that crieth in the wilderness, Prepare ye the way of the LORD, make straight in the desert a highway for our God. ⁴ Every valley shall be exalted, and every mountain and hill shall be made low: and he the rough places plain: ⁵ And the glory of the LORD shall be revealed, and all flesh shall see it together: for the mouth of the LORD hath spoken it.*

Who is the voice that crieth in the wilderness? Whose mission was it to *make straight in the desert a highway for our God?* The man who was beloved by Christ, the cousin of the Lord, John the Baptist! Look at the prophetic description of the coming of God, the coming of our Lord Jesus without a shadow of a doubt this shows and points to the equality of the Oneness of the Father and Christ. But this is only one of the scriptures that I am bringing forth before your eyes. Tradition is created by men, even Satan to divide and to continually pull you away from Christ, the way to everlasting life. For the work of your hands leads to death, but if you work by the Spirit you shall be prosperous, blessed going in and coming out, and in the field my brothers and sisters. I come not to bash you, but to break the spirit of tradition so that you may not *follow after the traditions of men, the rudiments of this world, but after Christ* to help you see that Light that shines so brightly before your eyes. I come in the Name of the Father, and of the Son, and of the Holy Spirit in Jesus Mighty Name to declare the One True God to you that you may be set free from the legalistic, systemic, traditional way of man and follow the Way of Life and Freedom, and receive His Whose yoke is *easy*, and Who's burden which is *light*, and not hard to bare.

Let's skip over to Isaiah 42:8-9,12-17, and 21: [8] **I *am* the *LORD*:** that is My Name: and **My *Glory I will not give to another, neither My Praise to any graven images*.** [9] *Behold, the former things are come to pass, and new things do **I** declare: before they spring forth **I** tell you of them.*

[12] *Let them give glory unto the LORD, and declare His Praise in the islands.* (Read at this closely my brethren.) [13] *The LORD shall come forth as a Mighty Man, He shall stir up jealousy like a man of war: He shall cry, yea, roar: He shall prevail against His enemies.* [14] *I have long time holden My Peace; **I have** been still, and refrain Myself: now I will cry like a travailing woman, **I will** destroy and devour (all) at once.* [15] **I will** *make waste mountains and hills, and dry up all their herbs; and I will make the rivers islands, and I will dry up the pools.* [16] *And I will bring the blind by a way that they not have not known: I will make darkness light before them, and crooked things straight. These things will I do unto them, and not forsake them.* [17] *They shall be turned back, they shall be greatly ashamed, that trust in graven images, they that say to the molten images, Ye are our gods.* [21] *The LORD is well pleased for His righteousness' sake; He will magnify the law, and make it honourable.*

With all honesty, who is this describing? Who is speaking here? The answer, you may be afraid to admit is Christ Jesus the Servant of the Lord, the Mighty Man is the Lord Jesus who ascended and descended into the depths to fill all things by the Spirit of God, which is His *Own Spirit*. Let them who have eyes see, and let them who have ears hear the word of the Lord for He spoke of His coming of His entrance, if you will, into the earthly sphere on earth as a man. Did Jesus, *the LORD* stir up jealousy? Yes! Look at the deep indignation of the Pharisees and how they plotted against Him to kill Him, because He did not look the part, or like them, did not follow the traditions that *they* had set forth. And for that He was ridiculed, hated, because He did not move by the spirit of tradition, but rather the Spirit of Him then that created the heavens and the earth. Oneness is hard to understand at first because in your carnal mind my friends, you think, "How can Jesus, the Son of God be the

Father? Being here at up there at the same time? He's His Son!?" Think not with the mind of the flesh, but with the mind of the Spirit of the Father. For those who are of the flesh will mind the things of the flesh, and those that are of the Spirit will mind the things of the Spirit. I pray that you see these errors in your doctrine my friends for the Father and the God of heaven and earth is not limited by any law that He has set forth(*or He wouldn't be God otherwise if He was bound by laws! But because He outside the laws of time, and the realm of men, above and outside the things that He created, this makes Him God!*), as in the law of the make up of man, nor is His power restrained, for we must not put our God in a box and think that He cannot work in many different ways. For yea, as the famous quote says, "God works in mysterious ways."

Look at the words of the Lord Jesus, *"I AM the Way, the Truth, and the Life, and no one can come to the Father, but by Me."* Because Christ is the Heavenly Father that descended and manifested in the flesh we can only reach Him *by Him. Helping is to* return to the True Image of God through Christ, *the Godhead*, Who was the great image of *the Invisible God* the glory of the Everlasting God being revealed through Him by the power of God*, see Romans 1:18-23, also Colossians 1:15-19.* See this my friends let your eyes be opened don't shut this book until you have reached a clear mind, along with what I say to you follow the scriptures my friends! Follow not the traditions of men, nor the rudiments of this world but after Christ, the Father, for as He saith He will not abandon you and will show you plainly of His Father, of Himself, who He had sent. The LORD Jesus Christ came by a way not known unto man, and that is the Holy Spirit of God manifesting forth as a mighty man in the flesh, taking upon sin, teaching and healing by the power in His Hands, so that you may find salvation in Him alone for remember this for *the Godhead dwelleth in Christ bodily*, Amen and Hallelujah to the Holy One of Israel!

Look again to John 14 in that same words that he spoke, *"If ye had known me, ye should have known my Father also: and from henceforth ye know him, and have seen him."* So clearly we·can see that the appearance, stature, the Spirit of Jesus Christ(*see John 3:34*) is indeed the make up and the equality of the Father God in Heaven, for they are indeed One as we should be in *Him* brothers and sisters. We are called unto One Body, One Spirit, and serving One Lord(*Ephesians 4:4-6*) with that one faith in Jesus Christ, one baptism in the name of the LORD Jesus Christ(Acts 4:12), the Maker of the heavens and the earth(Colossians 1:15). Amen.

I'd like to conclude this with a final scripture to help you see the Spirit of the Father in Christ(this does include the Holy Spirit for God is a Spirit and that same Spirit was in the Man that was Christ.) for Who is He is to you and the attributes and the genius of our Mighty King! Flip to Isaiah 43:10-12, let's go!

*[10] Ye are my witnesses, saith the LORD, and My Servant Who I have chosen: that ye may know and believe Me, and understand Me(when I say) that I AM He:(look at Jesus our Lord and Savior, the Christ confirm the Title of His Deity, I AM He when Judas Iscariot betrays his Lord into the hands of men.) before Me there was no God formed, neither shall there be after Me. [11] I, even I, I am the Lord, and beside Me **there is no(other)saviour.** [12] I have declared, and have saved, and I have shewed, when there was no strange god among you: therefore ye are my witnesses(those that know and understand will comprehend the meaning of this when I declare) saith the LORD, that I AM God. [13] Yea, before the day was I AM He; and there is none that can deliver you out of My Hand: I will work, and who shall let it?(or hinder it? Definition from Scofiield Study Bible, KJV) [14] Thus saith the LORD, your redeemer, the Holy One of Israel; For your sake I have sent you to Babylon, and have brought down all their nobles, and the Chaldeans, whose cry is in the ships. [15] I am the LORD, your Holy One, the creator of Israel, your King.***(Look over in Mark 1:24 when the King of all principality casts out a demon, and the demon refers to Him as the Holy One of, or in God.)***

The Lord clearly states in this set of scriptures that there is no other God but Him! *There is none beside me, I know not any*, saith *the LORD God* of Israel. God knows who He is and needs not be told of His Deity, but He does like it when we refer to Him as He is and that is *the Holy One of God of Israel, the King of kings, the LORD, Lord of lords, the King of Glory, the Maker of heaven and earth,* He *is the Mighty Man that came and stirred up jealousy like a man of war* against the false doctrines the Pharisees and scribes, He is the One Who spoke and taught the mysteries of heaven so that we may know them according to our salvation in Christ! What is His Name? Not the Title, but *Christ Jesus* the Living God and Lord of Israel, Who is over all things *now* and in the world to come, Amen! For allow me to say this that those were not names back in the Old Testament, but merely the Deity's Titles as He saw fit to as we should refer to Him as our God, but His Mighty and Strong Name is *Jesus Christ*, who was and is to come. God came upon the earth to save you and I let's come together break bread and be filled with the fullness of joy by *Christ Jesus, the Holy One*. Amen, hallelujah!

I can conclude saying this my brothers and sisters, ye have created and formed a God after the One already existed and was Him they ye exalt separately from the Father. Do ye know not that the Son of God declared Himself to be God, the Maker and the King of Israel? The One Who declared authority over heaven and earth? Do ye not know that there is another that come in the name of God(claiming to be God and Christ) that will deceive, and he will try to conquer you in these last days? Listen and hearken unto my words for they aren't mine, but of the Father in heaven. Make haste! And be made complete, whole in the One Who Created you Who is the Father, and the Son of the Living God who ascended and descended to fill all things! Listen no longer to the doctrines of your mothers, fathers, ancestors, but rather hearken unto the voice of the Lord for He loves you, and wishes *not for you to perish for having a lack of knowledge* but rather have everlasting life in Him, Amen.

For ye shall be called troublemakers for not following their law, but t*he fear of the Lord is the beginning of all wisdom, and the knowledge of the holy is understanding(Proverbs 9:10)*. For you shall be called a blasphemer and many other things according to the law and the legalistic system according to that doctrine that you are under, but the LORD of Hosts saith unto you,

"Fear not my child for the words of men amount not to anything, but My words concerning you shall stand. Think not of where you will go, what you will say for I will be with thee and will comfort thee, for I have said that I will be the cause of what separates mothers from daughters,

sons from their fathers, brother from brother, because of the true belief in Me, for I am the God of Israel and I conquered death so that you may have eternal life, and you may abound in it for eternity. For death shall not touch you, for My Hand will keep you steadily on the path of righteousness for I am the end of all righteousness and I will ensure safety against those that oppose you to the very end when I come in the clouds. Amen. " saith *the Lord God of Israel* unto you whomever reads this book for some shall repent and come to the truth and some will not, but will continue in their practices of their tradition rather than denying themselves and hearkening unto the voice of the King. May God be praised forever and ever, for eternity, in this world and the one to come, Amen. For if you have read any of the scriptures that the Holy Ghost has lead me to put before you, you are without excuse. If you are not sure, I adjure you pray to the Lord Jesus and He will reveal Himself to you. But those of you whose hearts have become hardened at the *words of Christ*, I see that you pray as well for clarity for when that day comes for you it shall be either terrible or a joyous day. Study to show yourselves approved my friends. If you are afraid to ask your pastor a question is that really the will of God that you cannot go to your pastor because you are afraid to question the faith, and test the spirits as the King of kings demands? Think on these things, and let God tell you when to move. It is important to use Wisdom in these last and evil days because the spirit of the antichrist is among you, and is out to devour *this* is why the Spirit of Christ (or the *Holy Ghost)* is so important to be able to perceive in the spirit realm who is operating under what spirit, for the spirits that oppose Christ are cunning and deceptive, *never* underestimate the devil, never think that you are smarter than him for he was born before you and knows the ways of God, and the Word of God more than you think. Of course no glory is being given to him, but I am only going by the scriptures he is to be under our feet, whom we trample over. Keep yourselves humble before the Lord, and never forget Who's power that it is that is inside of you, for it is *not your own*. Amen.

Onto the last doctrine that is taught in richness and that is *monotheism Christianity.* Yes, it is rich in value to those who preach the gospel of Christ, but is it rich in value if the word of Christ doesn't support it? Let's compare it with the word of Christ.

Around the world, monotheistic Christianity is taught in the richness, because of the divine revelation of the mystery of Christ and Who He truly is. Is the power of God shown through this doctrine? Are we following the traditions and the rudiments of this world and men, or are they following the Way of God? Have they reached full revelation of Him Who was sent? Most important of all is Christ the center of this doctrine? Let's see, if we begin at the beginning of the beginning of man. God said and I quote (from the KJV *Logos)*, ' " Let *us* create men in our image, after our likeness.." ' Now from reading this you could first think that the Lord is speaking to different people or *deities*, but if you read in the next verse it quiets that notion of that thought process, [27] *So God created man in His Own Image, in the image of God created He him; male and female created He them.* So as we read we can gather that God created us and I quote directly from His Word, *in His Own Image.* (His Personal Image, as in Only He owns the right to call it *His.)*

Your probably still thinking, what about the *'us'?* Who was He talking to if it was only Him? We must remember that God is a counsel unto Himself, He does speak about Himself naturally as we humans do in *third person, third person present*(check out Exodus 34). And you must also remember that the King has preeminence, meaning that He is there before all things and has an amount of incredible understanding and foreknowledge of events and after they happen. We must gather that in this case by the Spirit of the Most High that, He *was* literally talking to Himself, but speaking to His Persons or Roles that would later be revealed to man. As in the Father, the Son, and the Holy Ghost.(*By the way,* this kind of information cannot and be given of myself, but was given by the King of Glory and Power the Genius. In no way shape or form was getting to this information easy, but letting the God of Grace teach you is the best way to allow you to grow mightily in Him.)

He knew Who He would become, and what image that He created for His creation. Also, because He had foreknowledge the Lord of Hosts understood that He would later become, or at least be revealed to us the man He was, the Lord Jesus Christ. As a monotheistic Christian believer you, may or may not understand that the LORD God Christ was always who He became to be, but as time went on He slowly but surely revealed Himself with a Wonderful display of Glory and fullness in His Son the Lord Jesus Christ. First and foremost the Holy Father God of Heaven and Earth, the Son of God, and lastly the Holy Ghost, and all other titles for the important titles that I just said here in between such as Wonderful Counselor, which is another title for the Holy Ghost(For Counselor means *paraklētos* in Greek, which also means *advocate*, which does pertain to Christ 1 John 2:1; Prince of Peace, for the Son, and lastly the Maker is the Creator of Israel or Holy One of Israel can pertain to the Father and He is claiming to be the source of their coming forward by Him or their *birth* if you will, Amen. There are a plethora of other titles for the Deity search the scripture for more! And glorify Him!) Let's continue in the scriptures of God, *the image of God created He him; male and female He created them.*

The LORD's image was utterly perfect in the beginning needed not single thing changed, we once were perfect in Adam and Eve at the beginning. Once we fell we *fell away* from the perfect stature of spirituality, and life that He created us to have. So with the foreknowledge of the events that followed after creation the LORD understood that we were *no longer* in His image or likeness(spiritually) and then we became in the image of Satan, taking upon the *flesh*(or *carnality)*. By Him having His Foreknowledge, He knew that He would have to show us once again back to His Image. Restore us to back to us our dominion and our relationship with Him. Let's skip over to the book of Romans, chapter 8:28-29 this is what it reads(have your spiritual eyes open my friends), *[29] For whom He **did foreknow**, He also did predestinate to be conformed(transformed, or changed back into)to the Image of His Son, that He might be the firstborn among many brethren? [30] Moreover whom He did predestinate, them He also called: and whom He called, them He also justified, and whom He justified, He also glorified.*

Ask yourself, look in the scriptures, 'Who is the Son?' Why would the God of Heaven Who is Mightier and more perfect than anyone prefer a separate Image from His Own that was perfect and *already* pleasing to

His eyes? Did He fail, so He said, "Your Image shall they be created in, no longer mine?" Nonsense! My dear friends, little ones, sheep of the Most High hear the voice and read the words of Your Shepherd. John 14:7-9,KJV, *⁷ If ye had known Me, ye should have known My Father also and from henceforth ye know Him and have seen Him. ⁸ Philip saith unto Him, Lord, shew us the Father, and it sufficeth us. ⁹ Jesus saith unto him, Have I been so long time with you, and yet hast thou not know Me, Philip? He that hath seen Me hath seen the Father; and how sayest thou, then, Shew us the Father?*

So God knowing that He could not in any way, shape, or form appear only in Spirit for He is a Divine Being, the Highest of high, the Mightiest of the mighty, the Holiest of the holy, purer than a virgin could ever be. So, He clothed(*Philippians 2:5-10)* Himself in that of a man, in our likeness. He made sure to abide by the Law that He had set forth in the beginning to have man made in His Own Image so He created His Son, Who is the Father in His Own Divine Image that He saw that was perfect in spiritual stature according to His Law. So with saying that since we understand that Christ is the Father, and the Father is Christ, and the Holy Ghost or *Spirit* is that *same as* the Father God of Heaven. *Now*, we can understand that Christ the Father is working and restoring us back unto His Own image and likeness. He gave us a plain view as men, as sons and daughters of God how to conform back unto the Image of God by denying ourselves, taking up your cross, and be conformed, or transformed back into the image of God who was in Christ.

We can see Jesus our God responding as God the Father here and was literally asking Philip, " Those of you who see Me should know Me, they know the Father and that I *AM* Him. That when you see Me you see have seen Him. How can you ask Me to show you the Father when *I AM already here?*" Do you see the Genius of God? Do you see the love, passion, and all that He hath done for you my brothers and sisters? As the book of Philippians described that He stripped Himself of visible Glory that He was clothed in so that He could come to see about His creation, to save and rescue us my brothers and sisters! He made himself of *no reputation, humbling* Himself, knowing that He was God(Philippians 2:5-9*)*, but yet and still held His peace to show you the Way to everlasting life, *living as a Son*, to show us *how to become the sons of God.* Amen(*John 1*)! Now, we understand that the Image of God is the same as Image of the Son of God for they are equally One Being working as if He was two separate beings! Our God is to be glorified to the Highest of high for the Miraculous work that He had performed and what He continues to do for us! Glory, glory, glory belongs to the One who sent the Lamb of God to die for the remission of sins, and to declare His Kingdom on earth! Hallelujah praise God in the Highest, shout Hallelujah when you have understood my speech. I have showed you scripture of the Oneness of the LORD that is Christ and the Father, but there is more to be discovered and understood. You may have understood already that He is One with the Father, but you must understand it not just at the surface but rather more profoundly in ways that you did not see before. So, when you are confronted by those who oppose this belief you can show scriptural evidence that Jesus Christ is the One and True God of the heavens and the earth and that He is Lord.

One thing that I should point out before I move forward was that it was God's *desire* that He restores direct relationship with man, or access to Him freely, so what did He do? He sent Himself *a Servant, a Mediator, a Holy One, and a King*. Revealing Himself to be the God of the Old Testament, a Father, that He might show man the *Way* back unto Himself through(or through Himself, because no Glory is given *any other God, nor is the praise but only to the God the Father of Heaven and Earth! Amen!)* His Son Christ Jesus. Why do you continually call Him the *Son of God* if He is God, why not just call Him God? Well, my friends I could say this to you He is *simply* both, but it is *highly* important that when speaking of the Christ that in your conversation and confession(although saying that He is God is also important but), when you are admonishing each other that you do somewhere address and confess Him as *the Son of God*. Why? This is simply what it means, that *God manifested in the flesh, and that He still continues to do so(these words here are good to confess along with saying, "Jesus Christ is the Son of God")*. Confessing Him as the *Son of God* represents the Redemptive work that He completed as the man that He prophesied that would come(*Isaiah 42,KJV*), that God appeared in the flesh to save man, that God completed His work as He said He would, being the perfect sacrifice to save humanity, Amen. This is where it gets even deeper my friends, if he is not able to confess Jesus as the Son of the Living God, or completely dismisses that Christ even existed then he is an antichrist(or has the spirit of him inside of him, working by that evil spirit) and is a part of the coming apostasy church(*is already in formation, WARNING*). The devil, Satan, is not able to confess this mighty act, nor will he because that is reverencing God and His power that He was able to do so and He did. Test the spirits little ones and don't be afraid to because the spirit of the antichrist(LGBTQ community, who opposes and attacks the way of God, influencing the perversion of the creation of God, school shootings, all types of murders, different ways in our government, and other countries setting the stage for the true antichrist to step forward, so *keep watch and make God, the True God, Christ Jesus, your One and Only Stronghold, not friends, nor family, boyfriends or girlfriends but the Spirit of Christ who is on the right hand of God Interceding for you day and night, 24/7)* is already at work within the world as our brother John in *1 John 4:3*. Church *be ye sober, and vigilant my brothers and sisters* because at any time you fall asleep that spirit could attack and try to destroy the work of Christ that is at work in you and what you have already done, be *very, very* careful! That is why it is so important to *pray without ceasing* my friends you won't regret it, this way you are getting a spiritual "*check up*" on yourself and those that are around you. Keep watch in *Jesus Mighty Name! For the time is near for the Husbandman to return and claim His Bride. Amen.*

Do ye understand that the Spirit of God is the same as the Spirit of Christ? Do ye understand that the Holy Ghost is the power of the Spirit of God in Christ? We see clearly from scripture at the point that Christ is One with the Father, we see this in the intercessory and priestly prayer that prayed over His Disciples read here in John 17:11,20-21. He says this many times in every one of the Gospels, but in John's book is shows a more intimate setting. This reveals the King as the Servant coming forth for His people petitioning the needs and the desires of His Will to be done by the Father Whose will is identical, or *one*. We can understand that God is able to speak and to counsel, even reason with

Himself what is best for His People(*just as you do each and everyday my friends*). As the Son and the Servant of God He petitioned and prayed to God the Father, in supplication making His requests known to God for His Disciples. As God He reasoned and spoke to Himself, clarifying and speaking the things that He once had hidden with preeminence now shining forth today(that we'd be *one* just as He and His Father are indeed *One, in One Body, operating under One Spirit, serving One Lord. Ephesians 4:4-6*), Amen.

Hallelujah! Ye see now that the Father and the Son are One indeed, but the Holy Ghost, Who is He? Let's search the scripture my friends for the Holy One is an important One to know and understand Who exactly He is, for He is the completion of salvation and in the entrance into the newness of Christ following spiritually and reaching that *Image* that God wants us to return to, Amen.

Let's begin, returning the very profound and powerful scripture *Isaiah 9:6 KJV,* *⁶ For unto us a child is born, and unto us a son is given: and the government shall be upon His Shoulder: and His Name shall be called Wonderful, Counsellor, the mighty God, the everlasting Father, the Prince of Peace*. I see to it that you pay attention to the titles Wonderful, and Counsellor for they are the importance of what leads me to the next scripture, 1 John 2:1-2. Here it John the Baptist states under the power of the Holy Ghost flow by the Spirit of God, ' " *My little children, these things write I unto you, that ye sin not. And if any man sin, we have an **advocate** (along) with the Father, Jesus Christ the righteous: And He is the propitiation for our sins: and not for ours only, but also for the sins of the world."*' If ye recall my friends, and perceive the words that were written as the Lord Jesus Christ hath me to reveal to you that the words *advocate* stems from Greek word *parakletos* which translates to the word *Comforter*, and you've caught it rejoice! Allow me to further explain why the scripture *Isaiah 9:6* ties in with 1 John 2:1-2. I asked that you would keep the Titles Wonderful and Counsellor in your mind while reading the next scripture.

I have a question for you my friends, what you counselor's do? What is their main purpose? I have the answer, to comfort, to provide a way, discuss your issues with them, and to bring for a solution for you.

Recall little ones, *His Name shall be called Wonderful, Counsellor.* Jesus promised a *Comforter* did He not? He knew that the True Way for His creation to revert back to the Image of Himself would be through His Spirit, moving in a way that was not known by the *blind men, and that is the cleansing by fire.* Because of sin did we lose the Image of God, and through fire would we go through to reach once again to reach the Image of the Son of God as God predestined(Romans 8:28-29). Notice, God, Jesus the Son of God, the Holy Spirit (*or Holy Ghost*) all are referred to as *He.* Recall the Words of the Father, " *Yea before the **day**(that was to come in His appearance on earth) was **I AM He**."(Isaiah 43:13)* The words of the Son in His answers to the Jews, " *I said therefore unto you, that ye shall die in your sins: for if ye believe not that **I AM He**, ye shall die in your sins. "* Recall brothers and sisters what the LORD said as clear as day in Isaiah 43 that He, God the Father, was indeed the Servant that *He* was sending to rescue the earth. Also, look here when Jesus addresses the Holy Ghost as He, " *Howbeit when he, the Spirit of truth, is come, he will guide you into all truth: for he shall not speak of himself; but whatsoever he shall hear, that shall he speak: and he will shew you things to come.*
He shall glorify me: for he shall receive of mine, and shall shew it unto you. "

But to continue the Lord goes onto say that *beside(s) Me there is no saviour.* So with saying that how can Jesus the Christ receive the title of Lord and *Savior* if God the Father already clarified and said that there is no other Savior *besides Him?* There can't or else our Holy Father would be lying! That's preposterous! Our God is not a man that He shall never repent nor lie(*Numbers 23:19*), because the LORD God the Father of Heaven claims this Title He then later in that scripture that He *has indeed* saved before, and showed us a great deal of things so perceive *and* understand that the LORD Jesus Christ *is He,* Amen.

Let's not forget the Holy Ghost, the one who came and baptized by fire and filled the disciples with the fulness of the LORD, that is *Christ(Colossians 1:10, 2:10).* When we see the Holy Ghost, *He* is spoken about by Jesus, calling Him *the Comforter. He* would later receive *the things* of Jesus, for they weren't to be of His Own and reveal things to the disciples of the Father and Who Christ was and is, and also will *remind* the disciples of all the things that Jesus had spoken unto them. We can see that Jesus Christ *is* the *Comforter, knowing and reminding yourself from Isaiah 9:6* that *He* is the Wonderful Counselor, 1 John 2:1 the *advocate*, the *parakletos* for He confirms it here, "*But the* **Comforter, which is the Holy Ghost**, *whom the Father will send in My Name(because the Holy Ghost, the Father, and the Son will only respond to the One Name), He shall teach you all things, and bring all things to your remembrance, whatsoever I have said unto you.*" Friends let your eyes be opened and understand what the Father here teaches you in scripture clearly (*if you allow yourself to pay* **close** *attention*) who *He* is, and that *is God the Father, the Son, and the Holy Ghost.* Perceive and understand this my friends for the Father speaks to you, giving you clear insight of His Deity, and *wishes for you not to perish for a lack of knowledge of these things.*

(*Hosea 4:6, My people are destroyed for lack of knowledge: because thou hast rejected knowledge, I will also reject thee, that thou shalt be no priest to me: seeing thou hast forgotten the law of thy God, I will also forget thy children.*) I ask you my friends do not reject this knowledge of the Savior for He loves you so much and adjures you **not** to follow the rudiments of this world, or the traditions of men. Be He would rather you follow His Way through His Son, the Servant, the Only Savior, *which is Him.* One God and Father of All, One Spirit and Lord Who is over all in, through all, and above all. My friends allow His Knowledge, the *same* mind that was in Christ to dwell within you by the Spirit of Him who raised Christ from the dead. This what I have said unto you brings me to my last set of scriptures, let's come to an agreement and be the One Body that Christ *prayed* unto the Father for, just as *they were One* (*see in John 17:8-11,21-23).*

Let's go to Romans 8:8-13,

   [8] *So then they that are in the flesh cannot please God.*

⁹ But ye are not in the flesh, but in the Spirit, if so be that the Spirit of God dwell in you. Now if any man have not the Spirit of Christ, he is none of his.

¹⁰ And if Christ be in you, the body is dead because of sin; but the <u>Spirit is life</u> because of righteousness.

¹¹ But if <u>the Spirit of him that raised up Jesus from the dead dwell in you, he that raised up Christ from the dead</u> shall also quicken your mortal bodies by <u>his Spirit that dwelleth in you</u>.

¹² Therefore, brethren, we are debtors, not to the flesh, to live after the flesh.

¹³ For if ye live after the flesh, ye shall die: but <u>if ye through the Spirit do mortify the deeds of the body, ye shall live.</u>

This needs to be understood that God is a Spirit so we must worship *Him in Spirit and in truth, that is* in the essence of Who He is. The very nature of Who God was and is Christ, having the Spirit of Perfection only *from* the Spirit of God the Father *in* Christ. The reason I say the Spirit of Perfection(*even excellence, check out the book of Daniel those that opposed him recognized that there was an excellent Spirit within him.*) is to include and remind you of the will of the Father to return us back to, or conform us *back into* the *Image of God*. Then, with saying that my friends to the only True Way to Worship the Lord God is in *is to worship Him in Truth, **that is*** in truth of Who He is. We cannot worship the True God if we have not received the *True revelation* of *Who* God was and is. This is highly important my friends, look closely perceive *and* understand, let these questions ring in your mind daily if you are still hardened in the heart and *still* wish not come to the truth, for there are warnings in these questions. *Would you rather test what you believe to be sure, and save yourself from a burning hell and condemnation? If you have not received the True revelation of the mystery of Christ along with God, what spirit, who, what are you worshiping? Is the thought of pleasing man more important to you than pleasing God? Are the traditions of men causing you to be afraid to convert to what you know to be the Truth?* I come to tell you **this day**, that whom the *Son* sets free is free indeed! Be not bound by the traditions of men no longer, for their ways lead to hell!

Christ's work equals salvation for you! Do ye not know that He rebuked those who were legalistic and systemic?! He trampled over the spirit of tradition! Men need to have structure in order to function, but let me remind you that there is a Way to the Truth, that brings Life through His Works! I am bringing a rebuke to the systemic individuals who shut up heaven to those who needs to access it. I perceive in the Spirit by the Power of God that those of you that *will* read this are anointed by God, *highly anointed*, and those that are "*above*" you have shut up heaven and the access of God to you! I break their hold and their deception off of you by the power of the Holy Ghost! Satan you must leave them for they are indeed *God's chosen*! (When you read this you feel a shift happen! If you feel lead to do so, read this aloud with the voice of triumph in your home, declaring your freedom from tradition, Amen!) Hallelujah! Praise the God Almighty for His Power is great and has reached down to pull you out of the snare of Satan! Shout with the voice of a warrior who has just gotten the victory! Shout down the wall of *Jericho*(*tradition*), whom the Son of God by the Father has set your free from! Thank God!

Let's wrap this up in Jesus Name that ye may know your foundation! Look back at the verses in Romans 8, one thing that you should ask yourself is this, *How is having the Spirit of God the Father not enough to be His? Why is the Spirit of Christ so important to being the LORD's?* Recall back to Colossians 2:9, [9] *For in him dwelleth all the fulness of the Godhead bodily.* (*Talking about Christ Jesus!*) We should be able to conclude at this point and time that Christ the Servant *is* the One and True God! For in Him dwelleth the Godhead bodily! What is the Godhead? It is the makeup of *the Father, the Son, and the Holy Ghost*, all dwelling in *One* body of Christ! He is One with the Father, One with the Spirit of God, and He is the Son, who has power and authority over the heavens and the earth! *Who is the image of the invisible God*? That is Christ He was Emmanuel, who was and is, "*God with us*", how can He be separate from the King while being ***the King of the Jews***? How can He not be *one* with the Father if *He* declared it? Is He a man that He shall lie? No. For there was no guile found in His mouth! Nor can there ever be, for He is the Truth, the first and the last, the beginning and the end, His Word has come true and every bit of it. If *He* be a liar how is everything how it is? How has everything that *He the Mighty Prophet* said would come to pass? Ask yourself these questions my friends for God is not a liar, but men are! Stop desiring a King when you already have One, stop searching for someone to mentor you when you have a *Counselor*, stop lifting up and praising your pastor when you have only *One to Worship and to give glory* to!

For I say this unto you in confidence, and by the power of God that has been placed upon me to write this book to you, my friends, that everyone who has one mind in tradition are following men, and listening to them, and following them only will prove to be a snare! For I prophesy unto you that when the wrath of God commences doth thou think that your "shepherd" will save your life over his? The answer is no, he will not why? He will be running for his life to save his own because his heart has become like the *wicked servant,* and denied the power, the authority, even the knowledge of God, by preaching and *"giving you words of wisdom"* by their own conscience and not by the *Spirit of God.* Confess Christ as Lord and Savior today(This confesses that He is *God, and the One that He sent as the Servant. Completing the redemptive work for you and me in human form as God.)* for in you is the spirit of Satan, your father, and he cannot confess *Jesus Christ is the Son of God* because like I stated before he will not give God glory for the work He did for man, coming *as* a *man.* Amen. Be no longer hindered by traditions, by laws, nor rudiments of the world and men, but I adjure you, *follow God* my friends, be ye separate and conform to the *Image of the Son of God* who was and is *the Invisible Image of the Begotten God.* Let not the faces, nor the knowledge of men and what they think about God stop you from coming to the truth my friends. Know this, that Jesus the God of heaven and the earth invites you to join Him and He says, *"Come, My children."*

We now know and understand at this point that Christ is *one with the Father* not only in Person, but also in Spirit. Also, that ye cannot have the Spirit of God without having the Spirit of Christ. To have not the Spirit of Christ makes you not son of God, or *one of his own* for we are complete in *Him.* To tie the bow on this in the scriptures, let us jump to another scripture there is never too much Word that can be placed within you (*by the Spirit of God of course*). Skip over to Ephesians 4:4-6, these will help you reach an understanding, I have faith in God that He will help you to understand this speech of *His, that is of the Truth*. Ephesians 4:4-6 states, and I write,

> *⁴ There is one body(Christ), and one Spirit(that is the Spirit of Christ which is valid to be one of God's), even as ye are called in one hope(Christ, the hope of glory) of your calling;*
> *⁵ One Lord(Jesus, LORD, LORD GOD), one faith(that there is one God), one baptism(and that is in Jesus Name, in which the Lord commanded Matthew 28:19),*
> *⁶ One God and Father of all, who is above all(John 3:31), and through all(1 Corinthians 2:16), and in you all(Philippians 2:5).*

Look at this my friends the Father claiming ownership of the body of Christ, the Spirit that was in Him, and the Lordship that He was titled upon the earth *and* in the heavens. For the LORD spoke, "*All power(authority) is given unto Me over heaven and earth.*" For this power was already His to begin with friends, but as the King always loves to clarify and to declare it has been *given* to Him by Him, Amen. For there is not three gods, nor there is two, but One God and we see that here *little ones*. Recall in Romans 8, *if so be that the Spirit of God dwell in you. Now if any man have not the Spirit of Christ, he is none of his.* Are there two Spirits that we should move by? Are we supposed to be of two bodies, *even* three? No, my friends let those who perceive *see*, and let those who hear *listen*, there cannot be two nor three spirits but only One. For the scripture declares it: *One Body, and One Spirit*, are we called to in the hope of our calling. One LORD, Lord doth rule over us, One God and Father created us whose *same* Spirit was in Christ who hath ascended and descended, *Whose* Spirit *and* Power (if ye had received it through the power of His Spirit manifested through tongues only) is above all, and through, *and in you all*. Praise God! You no longer have to serve two masters, or *three*, but Whose *Power* and *Genius* reigns in the Godhead, Christ Jesus, the Son of the Living God, Amen.

Lastly, just to make *sure* that you may know in full the revelation and have the foundation you need for God to build upon for yourselves and those who will come out of the churches of tradition, from the *gossip houses*, that you may admonish one another with the revelations of the mysteries of God in Christ. That *He the Father, that He the Son, that He the Holy Ghost* is *Elohim*. For the Name, *Elohim*, is plural, meaning "gods", but at the end of the six letter words in *him, elo-* many, *-him* indicating One *Man or Being*. The Name of the Spirit is Jesus the Christ. For the God that we serve deals in plurality, is not subject to one way to move, remember He is omnipresent, omniscient, and omnipotent. But He loves to reveal Himself One Way at a time, and when you have revelation of each Way, it all leads back to the mind of Christ, whose is the Father's Who is of the Holy Ghost of God. Amen! *Let the True Church of God, who has built a temple for Him to reside in say, Amen and Amen, may the God of both the heavens and the earth be praised forever and ever, Selah.*

2. *Receiving Power from on High through Baptism*

Rejoice! For ye have made it to chapter two! God has revealed Himself to you, His Person through Christ, Who is the *same* Spirit that ascended and descended, Amen. For God is a God of revelation and loves to reveal Himself to us, only if you will *let* Him. God is not a forceful God, but honors the gift that He gave us according to His Own Deity and

Image, allowing us to keep the godly image, if you will of *free will*. Please understand this, that our God stretches His Hand forth towards you, and His mouth is open to speak to you for He has spoken and will continue to speak to those whom *He* wishes for He is the Way to *everlasting life*, Amen.

Listen friends, brothers and sisters of the faith I adjure you that you pray for your leaders, that you keep them holstered up in prayer. Also, your other brethren in the faith for the evil one wishes to *kill, steal, destroy and seeketh whom he may devour.* There is a lot of pressure that comes with speaking the *truth of the faith freely*, but the power that is from on high is greater than the powers that are working here on earth and in the spirit realm. I need you to understand young ones that this is indeed a spiritual battle, not per-say a physical one. For the LORD Jesus condemned and rebuked the practice of glorifying the work of hands as in doing the things of tradition *according to men*, because *you want to receive praise from men rather than God and heaven*(John 12:43). For the Church and its make up have now turn into a material, or carnal thing when it was never intended to be this way, for if we are supposed to turn away(completely doing a 180, while some do a 360 degree turn landing in the exact same place, because they choose to remain in their sin) from the desires and wants of sin, because we are *stepping into the Spirit*. Also, being baptized in *Him*.

The Image of God in the Church has been corrupted once again like Adam and Eve, and like a very first brother, Cain, we are giving sacrifices unto the LORD that He is rejecting, *because* they are not what He asked for and declared. I say this to whomever reads this for I perceive some of your thoughts when you read this, *Why does it have to be that way? Why couldn't the loving God receive what Cain was sacrificing?* Well, friends that is why the King placed me here to teach you what He has taught me concerning this. First and foremost, you must understand your place then the place of God. *Who are you to judge, or make a rebuttal to the LORD of Hosts?* For He is only *Holy and Just One*, ye are from *the dust of the earth, and to the dusts of the shall ye return(Genesis 3:19).* Know your place people of God, understand where we as a people come from and Who exactly our Creator is. You may feel some way about the things I just said, but think on this, *Would ye dare utter a rebuttal against your earthly father or mother?* I think not, for you know the hand of Momma or Dad would come across the face if you talked back! If our Father and Mother chastise us with paddles, belts, and their hand how much more can the Lord do to chastise us and make sure that we understand what we did wrong?

Think of God the Father and respect Him just as ye would your mother and father here on earth, for when ye honor them ye do *honor Him(see number five of the Lord's commandments in the book of Exodus whence they were given to Moses, Amen)*. Yet when ye honor Him, your honor will be higher than that of your parents for He is your Creator, First Love, your Holy One *and* Father, Amen. May God bless you for your obedience if you have done these things for the times are just as the Word of God spoke of in the *perilous times, for they shall be disobedient to their parents and unthankful*(see 2 Timothy 3:2). May God keep you in that stature of obedience that you may grow as a flower, and rising when *His Light* touches you, Amen.

The times are upon us my friends, and while reading this you may say, *My Grandma and Grandpa(or whomever it may be)always said that, they've been saying it for years ever since I was a kid.* But friends I ask you that you would step out from the spirit of the flesh to perceive, and *see* that the times are *truly* upon us my friends! Yes, we have had earthquakes before in different places, but not in this kind of frequency, let your eyes be opened. Some of you may have read 2 Timothy 3:2, do ye see that all these things are true? Every. Single. One. This is no coincidence, *not just by chance*, but was declared and set forth by *the preeminence and the foreknowledge of Christ.* You Christians who, say that you are Christians believe not in the last days, in the wrath that God will pour upon this world and nation because of sin. A|re you a believer then? Do you *fear the God of heaven?* You should *fear* Him as in you *highly respect and adore Him,* but you should also *fear* as in you are afraid in trembling as well for to fear what men can do to you is nonsense, but *He is the One who can destroy your physical body, and send your soul to hell(Jesus said this of Himself, the Father in the Gospels, see Matthew 10:28).*

But does the God of heaven, the Holy Father want us to be *afraid* of Him, of course not my friends! He loves us! Just as a father here on earth loves his child and wants him not to be afraid to ask him questions as he grows, so does the King of kings, our *Holy One of God.* Yet forget not to respect your Heavenly Father for who He is, but also reminding yourself that you have direct access to Him through His Son, Christ, and by Christ the Father, Amen. Praise and let us adore God for His Love for His People!

Just as a Father loves His children, and wants to see them succeed, also wanting see Himself within us just as any father does. He wants to see in imprint *on* us. How do we become *like* God, how do we return, conform to the Image of His Son? Do we just go up to the altar and pray, repent, be baptized in water? Is that it? With many traditions and religions, a lot of people believe truly that, that is the last step in salvation. That is praying, repenting(acknowledging your sin and confessing the to the Father), accepting the Lord your Savior, then *baptism in water*. That this is the completion of salvation. As I said before my friends I have been sent by the Father to declare His Truth, not mine, only going by His Word that has He spoken, and tell what He performed because it does indeed pertain to your salvation. *You are His children*, and you deserve to know the *Truth* of *His Power, and His Willingness to give it to whom He sees fit*. I speak to you of a power that is said to be a myth to some, and something that isn't necessary to some people. I speak of the power that was poured out and displayed by the LORD Jesus Himself, through the out pour of His Spirit on His disciples, the filling, and the *power of the Holy Ghost*, the speaking of other tongues.

This knowledge has been shut up to many of you by your pastors, by the traditionalist, the legalistic systemic "christians", or the scribes and the Pharisees of today. That same spirit of hinderance is working today my friends and many of you are victims of this crime, some of are wolves who have been sent to put a hold on the knowledge of power reaching the sheep to overthrow you. I *see* you, and you need to understand their either you need to move or *you shall be moved*. Sheep, hear the voice of your True Shepherd, Who is the Door to safety and refuge! This power that I speak of is only given by the Holy Ghost Himself, your Lord and Savior Christ Jesus, I ask of you to read the words of the Father through what I say to help break this down to you. First, you need to see that you are a sinner, and you need to recall what that actually means, and understand exactly what you were born *into*. Let me tell you, when you we born we inherited the same spirit that our *father,* Adam, received once he fell, condemning humankind to an eternal life in hell. This spirit that was unleashed upon the land was the spirit of death, which is the after effect of sin, the *wages of it. But*, we have a *Savior*, and that *is Christ*, who was sent by *His Father* to save us from these very sins that we have done, and *will* do in the future.

The reason, I say this is so that you is so you know that the devil, or your father has tainted you, but my friends all the blame cannot go to him, *because* he doesn't make you do anything that you don't want to do friends. Just as everyone else ye must repent for your sins as well, just as I did, in no way shape or form am I exclude in any manner of when it pertains to sin. I speak to you the words of the King. Hear this *and* listen, because we have been born into this, and have committed sin against our Father, we have been separated from Him and it has pulled you away from His Love and the knowledge of Him, and His existence. It has brought us to a state of rebellion, an uprising against our Lord, which the devil orchestrates, yet like I said he cannot make you do something that you don't agree to. I hope that this has knocked you down, or better to say humbled you so that you know not just your position but all of our positions that some of us once had(and not to say that as believers we won't sin, but willingly is something that the Lord helps us to refrain from, and also the ones we do subconsciously we should still repent for.) back before we ever met the Lord Jesus Christ.

Humble yourselves before the Lord Jesus and understand that your knowledge, your PHD's, your biblical school doesn't match the teaching and the knowledge of the LORD GOD of heavens and the earth, A man can only teach carnal things and try to make them fit his knowledge, but the LORD God Almighty can teach *and* give Wisdom on the material(*or earthly*) things as well as the heavenly(or *spiritual*)things. Biblical college doesn't teach you, the things of the spirit, only God can do that, when you come out you say, "How can you teach me? I know 90% of the Bible." but yet and still come out lacking the knowledge of the holy things and the mysteries of Christ and heaven. You still come out not having the full revelation of the Father and Christ and the Spirit of God and their oneness, and still deny the power of God that is manifested through tongues. Why? Because carnally born were you born, and carnally minded you will be, not understanding the things of God because ye were taught by men rather than God. Yes, you may have credentials in the material world, but do the heavens and its Creator *know* you in the Spirit? Have ye been rewarded spiritually with the Holy Ghost with all the knowledge you have? Or are you like the scribes and Pharisees, who know the *law of God*, yet deny the power thereof? Have ye tried to make things fit your knowledge rather than denying yourself, and listen to the Father of hosts? Your knowledge doesn't matter here! God looks to teach those who want to be taught and those who have a teachable spirit. Not some who thinks they know everything! Humble yourselves before the Lord of Hosts!

With saying that my friends the power that I speak of is sent by the Spirit of the Servant who manifested and displayed the great *glory of God* to the eyes of His people. Let's look at the scripture and compare it to the knowledge of the carnally minded "Christians" of today. Flip to Acts 2:3-4,

> *¹ And when the day of Pentecost was fully come, they were all with one accord in one place.*
>
> *² And suddenly there came a sound from heaven as of a rushing mighty wind, and it filled all the house where they were sitting.*
>
> *³ And there appeared unto them cloven tongues like as of fire, and it sat upon each of them.*
>
> *⁴ And they were all filled with the Holy Ghost, and began to speak with other tongues, as the Spirit gave them utterance.*

Just as the Lord promised the power from on High, it came and just as I spoke about before that the LORD has preeminence and foreknowledge making Him the Almighty Prophet! This power can be and only manifested through tongues, and in that to say you have the Holy Ghost the evidence is the tongues given by the Holy Ghost. Many believe that the Holy Spirit can be given and the tongues come later. Let's look in scripture is that possible, is it true? Is it supported by scripture? You've clearly read Acts 2:3-4, that it happened immediately my friends, now let's go to the powerful story of Cornelius(*an Italian*) and his family.

Here's what is says in Acts 10:45-46,

45 And they of the circumcision which believed were astonished, as many as came with Peter, because that on the Gentiles also was poured out the gift of the Holy Ghost.
46 For they heard them speak with tongues, and magnify God.

You can see my brothers and sisters that the occurrence of the Holy Ghost brings tongues with Him, and you I hope can perceive and see what I have spoken and warned if ye have not the evidence of the Holy Ghost through the manifestation of the heavenly tongues given by Him that ye have not the Spirit of God in you. I apologize not, for if you were taught this, you can see that the scriptures and the Word of God disagrees with the notion that the Holy Ghost comes without the fire. I am not afraid in this manner for I know that many demonic spirits are aware of this and the doctrine of the Lord! And they think that they can cover up by saying, "I have the Holy Ghost, but He hasn't given me the tongues *yet.*" Or, "I speak in tongues only in private, because the tongues He has given me are meant for the privacy of Him and I." I rebuke that spirit of confusion, manipulation, and hindrance in the mighty Name of Jesus! You will not stop the move of God nor bring confusion for God is not the author of confusion, but the Author of Peace! For John baptized with water but the one that came after him baptized with *fire.* The demonic forces are afraid of the Lord, for His power and presence, the tongues terrify them, for the manifestation of tongues is the display of God's power upon His People. Look at how they cried out when they saw *Jesus,* because when they saw Him they saw *God,* and the power of the *Spirit* that was manifesting in Him! Remember that we are born not into the

Light, but into darkness, and we love it and just like Satan we fear the Light, but I say unto you little children fear not this power for it is given from on *High by the Father in Heaven Who has the Rightful seat in Power, Amen. Hallelujah!*

Some of you may still be in denial, for you are afraid of receiving this power, and still think that the Spirit of Christ dwells in you. Allow me to bring more scripture before your eyes that you may see the truth of God for yourself. *Amen.*

Our God when He gives something as valuable as the Holy Ghost, He does it with immediacy, not in delay. This is the confusion, and the unwillingness of man accepting the truth, and the unwillingness to deny themselves and accept the truth. Let's go to Acts 19:6-7,

⁶ And when Paul had laid his hands upon them, the Holy Ghost came on them; and they spake with tongues, and prophesied.
⁷ And all the men were about twelve.

Immediacy, immediacy, immediacy the Word of the Lord declares immediacy in this matter I could go on, but prayerfully by now I hope that you see the point that I am making by the *Holy Ghost*. Jesus said, " At that day ye *shall* know that, *I am* in my Father, ye in Me, and I in you." We see the fullness of the Godhead here! The Holy Ghost, that is Jesus Christ speaks as in foreshadowing the coming *promise of His Spirit* in man. Look closer my friends that are trying to understand and want the *seed embedded in the earth of your heart and not be as the seed being thrown on the stony ground.* See this, the Lord Jesus is claiming to be the Father in the second part of the sentence my friends, *I am in my Father,* then watch this He doesn't go to say that *He is in Me,* but, *ye in Me*(or you in Me), and lastly Him with(or being) the Father in us His People. *He is* speaking of the Great and Wonderful Counselor, He Who was the same that *ascended and then descended to fill all things* with His Spirit, Jesus Christ, Amen.

Again, I say let those who have an ear to hear let him hear, and those who have eyes to perceive and see, Amen. The Lord Christ is the Holy Ghost, the Wonderful Counselor or Comforter, He Who desires to dwell within you and give you power from on *High*, why? To give you power to endure the times that are coming, to trample over your enemies, to be able to cast out demons, to heal the sick, to teach the Gospel with accuracy *because* His Spirit is reminding you of what *He* said in *His Word*. This is the furnishing process to get you back to Image of Him Who raised Christ from the dead my friends, understand this, just as glass has to go through a process of *fire* in order to become clear and spotless. The same you in the Spirit to rid you of all stains of sin and evil you have done, in order to restore the Image of God back to you, that is why this is so important and also when that time comes He may not say to you, *"Depart from ye who work iniquity I never knew you."*

Scary are those words isn't it? They should be, especially if you think His Spirit dwells in you and it doesn't. These words may come as a shock, or a stumbling block to you, but if it helps you to turn from the traditions and rudiments of men then I will continue by the *Grace of God* to do so, *because I love each and everyone of you.* And I wish not for the Husbandman to call for us to come and just as the *five virgins* who went to get some oil because they had none. And I am sorry but if you are one of those who didn't get any oil while thou *couldst, ye cannot borrow any from mine nor anyone else's lest we have enough for ourselves.(see Matthew 25 to read about the ten virgins, Amen!)* This saddens my heart to see all this tradition running rampant through the church these days, and those who know the Word see and because they fear the *elders* they don't speak up, for I say unto you be not afraid of those who sit high and seem to cannot be touched for there *shall not go any stone unturned, saith the Lord.* The pegs of their pedestal will collapse by the Hand of the Lord in these days, because they themselves have run out of oil, and no longer have any anointing with them, and *just* the virgins are trying to *borrow from others.* Stepping up over one another to get to the top, to be the most anointed when none have any oil to give, but I say unto you my friends, to you *elders* that those you have shunned for questioning the doctrine you teach, and what spirit you teach of, are the same one's whose lamp is full of oil, and as ye fall by the Hand of the Lord, with that same Hand He shall rise those you have tried to sabotage on their way up. And you shall be sick of what the LORD God will do for them, for *your indignation and slanderous words against them* and *the anointing that God has placed upon them will cause defilement and blemish upon you.*

For it's not what goes into the body that defiles the body, because it goes to the belly and into the toilet my friends, but *what proceedeth out from him shall indeed defile him, saith the Lord God Almighty.*

Mark 7:14-16, *[14] And when he had called all the people unto him, he said unto them,*

[14] "Hearken unto me every one of you, and understand:

[15] There is nothing from without a man, that entering into him can defile him: but the things which come out of him, those are they that defile the man.

[16] If any man have ears to hear, let him hear."

So I adjure *elders*, and whoever speaks against those that are of God to hold your peace and take it to the altar, deny yourself, *your* pride, *your* indignation, repent for these for they are great sins against the Lord, and if you think you will get away with it you got another thing coming. If ye asked the question, *"Who are you to tell me anything? I am the elder."* You are correct that ye are an elder so then my question to you is, *"Why are you doing these things which I speak of?"*

I speak what the Lord God wants me to speak, and I do it with dependence and confidence in *Him only,* **never** myself because just like you I am a man and will remain that, and I am no lower or higher than you, and you are no higher or lower than me. For, I'd rather be questioned by you *elders* with your traditions, than be asked by the Lord, that is Christ, *"Why did ye not say what I wanted you to say My son?"* For, I'd rather not be questioned by the *Holy Ghost*, for I fear *Him* far more than I fear you men. For *He is my God*, and ye *are* my brethren, *He is my Rock*, you are stones along with me that builds His Temple, I am a piece of clay just like you.

So I adjure you *and warn* you step down from your pedestals, and repent! Make not yourself and your works idolized, make not it seem that you are the elite in the building that no one can have greater faith and can do greater works than you. Don't shut up heaven for those who desire to move in the direction of the Holy Ghost, suffer them not, for as I said before *if you do not move you will be moved.* For the Hand of the Lord Himself will knock down the pegs of your pedestal to wake you up and it will be hard to come back from that, why? Because ye were warned of your transgressions against the King and His people and did not act, but continued deceiving and manipulating, and for this your reward, and yea will it be great. Just as you sew greatly to manipulate the people, shouting your alms before men that they may see, greatly will it be measured unto you my people,(*I say this as humbly as I know by the Lord Jesus Christ) Amen and Amen.*

So, you may ask, *"Jordan, I understand all of what the Lord is saying through you, but how do I receive the Holy Ghost? Do I have to be baptized (in water) first?"* Well, my friends, the answer is *prayer and supplication unto the Lord Christ* and even *fasting as the Lord tells you.* And what you need to understand first before you can began praying for the Holy Ghost and the *evidence of it,* it to make sure you *understand* what you are *asking and pleading* for God to do. If you can recall, we see that it is power given from on High, by God, and it is power to do mighty works for the Lord, to teach, to minister, to prophecy, to preach the Word with the Fire of the Holy Ghost, to evangelize, to heal(*you may not be called to do all of these, but it is highly important that you follow God to know what you are chosen and called to do my friends, Amen*). This *is the oil in the virgin's lamps, this is the Indwelling of the Spirit of Christ* Who has done all the things that I listed. He has prophesied, ministered, did a great deal of healing, and teaching, and definitely preaching to the witnesses His Disciples and those who received the seed that He, the Sower, was planting.

Be not afraid, for yes the Holy Ghost comes with His own language, but look at this my brothers and sisters, and those of you who are trying to comprehend and are receiving this seed. The Holy Ghost brings a language from heaven just for you *personally,* individually we are given tongues to speak according to the Lord and His desire, and as He being the Mediator or the One you *groans with you, uttering things not known to man(Romans 8:26-27, see the Lord Christ who has the mind of the Spirit and is the One and Only Spirit of God, Ephesians 2:5).* So no other man on earth knows this language, and only heaven recognizes it, not even Satan who was an angel at one time *who did not keep his first estate(heavenly or angelic)*, doesn't understand or comprehend it. ***That***, is *why* he is afraid of it, *because* he doesn't understand the language of God and ultimately has to give up because we have such a powerful leverage over him by the *Spirit of God, not ourselves of course.* With saying that, those of you are of it and see what I am saying, *praise God the Most High!* For those of who don't allow me to say these words that'll hopefully quicken you to the Lord, and open your heart more to *Him.*

        Satan, is *so* cunning and evil, and so are the wolves that he has dispersed into the church, bringing tradition and lies into the *holy place of sanctuary*. What do you think that he has done to you? He has came into the minds of you "believers", you traditionalists, you legalistic systemic hypocrites, and has whispered these very words to you and you willingly believed it, "*You don't need to* **speak in tongues***(receive the Holy Ghost)* **to be saved***. You don't* **need** *the Holy Ghost to go to heaven. You don't need to* **speak in tongues** *in order to* **have the Holy Ghost***.*" Lies! Lies! And more *lies*! How can you believe such blasphemy? Have ye not read the scriptures and the *filling of the Indwelling of the Spirit of Christ* in the *True Believers*? *This* is why they were persecuted so greatly, not because they had the title of *Christians*, but because they had *the Spirit of the Lord* dwelling inside of them and Satan perceived it and caused men's hearts to become hardened, causing indignation in them, causing them to revile against the disciples. *Why?* Because he is afraid of the power of God, and even more so *God coming in his* territory and destroying it! Hallelujah! Look at what he has done to you and you let him! Because of your traditions you willingly *ignore and deny the power* thereof in the book of Acts, *then* not only that you *still* think that you have the Spirit of God dwelling on the inside of you when there was no sound neither is there any evidence! Deception and confusion my friends! Why? Because your traditionalistic *elders*, have turned the doctrine of God upside and have corrupted it to make you less radical, to contain and constrain you, so that they can do what? *Keep you bound*!

        Oh LORD God of Heaven! Have mercy upon those who have willingly twisted your doctrine to deceive your people, forgive these

Pharisees who deny the power thereof, forgive them that willingly work iniquity and try to still be holy! Forgive them that are hypocrites in the pulpit in the groups of the elders! For my heart is saddened at this and I ask you to extend your mercy upon these individuals who have corrupted your church that they may have a chance to return to You and do the mighty acts of God, **with the Indwelling of Your Spirit***, Amen and Amen.*

Satan has come through and *has killed, has stolen, and has destroyed!* And your elders, those who skip the part in acts in the beginning and only speak of what the disciples did, your parents who prevented you from asking any further questions about this matter, told you to forget about it, told you that it was a myth. You willingly let the dragon come in, destroy, steal, kill the spirits of those who want life to be quickened and are hungry for the Spirit of God, and rebuild and make a new home! You who read this! Look what you've done to your own people! Aren't you ashamed, for denying them *this power from on High?* I hope that you see your error here and that ye repent for the what you have done to your own! For heed to this warning that the Godhead warned! [5] *Jesus answered, "Verily, verily, I say unto thee, Except a man be born of water and of the Spirit, he cannot enter into the kingdom of God.* [6] *That which is born of the flesh is flesh; and that which is born of the Spirit is spirit."*

Ye cannot enter the Kingdom of God, **without** *the* **Spirit of God** *within you! Unless ye be* **born of water and Spirit** *ye cannot enter the Kingdom of God!* My heart aches at this crime that you have committed against so many people, how many years you've been lying to those you say you love, deriving them of this power that God wants to give! *How dare you stand in the way of the Most High God? Saying, "I shall do these things so that I may have a church where it's containable for I am the High Priest, and I don't want just anyone coming up after me." Again I ask, How* **dare** *you?!*

Going on my friends, understand and know this! *No flesh(our physical bodies, and of course sin!) will enter Heaven, only he that is born of water and Spirit will enter heaven!* I don't care if you went everyday to preach the Word of God on the corner! Or healed a sick woman, or casted out a demon in Jesus Name, *again I say the words of*

Christ our Holy One of God, "Except a man be born of water and of the Spirit, he cannot enter into the kingdom of God." For you will say, "Lord, Lord haven't we healed in Your Name, haven't we taught in your Name, haven't we cast out demons in your Name?" For He will reply in all Truth, *"I never knew ye: depart from Me, ye that work iniquity."* For the Lord here professes and declares that He will say these words *to whom He doesn't know you and those that work iniquity or lawlessness.* But you may ask, *How does the Lord not know me?* And I can simply say this to you my friend, because ye never *knew Him,* He never *knew you.* At this time it will be too late to receive His Spirit into you for you will have been judged! For He in the Spirit, Who is of Spirit will not recognize *Spirit,* but will recognize flesh which has not been cleansed *from iniquity because* you held yourself back from learning the truth and not accepting it for what it was and denying yourself.

Now, I clarified the part about the *Spirit by* the *Spirit of God,* to help you understand what the part simply means my friends, you don't have to pray for three months to figure out the answer after you have denied the answer plenty of times now ye know the truth, not by words but by *the words of the Father of Grace, Amen.* But what about the water part? What does that consist of? Is it the water baptism? Is it necessary for us to be baptized in water in order *to reach true salvation and righteousness?* Well, let's again as you know look in the scriptures of God, and what He spoke about concerning this, Amen. Let's look at Matthew 3:13-17,

13 Then cometh Jesus from Galilee to Jordan unto John, to be baptized of him.

14 But John forbade him, saying, I have need to be baptized of thee, and comest thou to me?

15 And Jesus answering said unto him, "Suffer it to be so now: for thus it becometh us to fulfil all righteousness." Then he suffered him.

16 And Jesus, when he was baptized, went up straightway out of the water: and, lo, the heavens were opened unto him, and he saw the Spirit of God descending like a dove, and lighting upon him:

17 And lo a voice from heaven, saying, "This is my beloved Son, in whom I am well pleased."

Don't be angry nor be filled with indignation, for the Lord of Hosts has brought you evidence and many answers included in one set of scriptures, concerning *the baptism of water* and the necessity *of it*, to do what? "*To fulfil all righteousness.*" Then right after He comes out from the water, John witnessed the Spirit of the Lord descending upon Him like a dove. *Amazing, Hallelujah!!* At that moment the *Son of God*, Jesus, the Christ, was verified to be *Him* in front of the eyes of men. I adjure you not to let your mind become carnal and think to yourself, "*Ha! Jesus didn't speak in tongues so I don't have to!*" You must read the scriptures! *In all thy getting get an understanding* most of all folks, for this is important for if ye are not careful you could lead many people to the depths, along with yourself my friend.

Don't allow Satan to cause you to be narrow minded, prayerfully you took some notes,(not saying that you have to of course) but do ye not recall Who the Lord that is Christ was? *He is Elohim, He is the Spirit of God manifested in bodily form, He would be the One to baptize us men in the fire of His Spirit(Matthew 3:11, John 1:33, go there and read this for yourself and I believe by the power of the Holy Ghost within me that you will perceive and see then believe!).* So to answer your question by the Spirit of Christ within me, He didn't need to speak in tongues, why? Because *He is the Holy Ghost, and He is the One that disperses His Spirit among men.* But remember my friends that when the Holy Ghost speaks through us, it is in the manifestation of tongues, *He the Spirit of Christ. Who is He? He groans and speak things that cannot be uttered by men.* Do you not think that heaven consists of it own language? Why do you think heaven recognizes it and moves on your behalf when you speak it my friends? That's not to say that they don't understand English just in case you thought that my friends, the Lord God created all languages, see when He destroyed the tower of Babel(*Genesis 11:5-9*).

Let's continue in the baptism of water, for Christ was baptized, even though He was and is *God* friends He was already *holy and just*, but I believe this to be true that He said and did those things for those who that would come after who had believe on Him. People like you and me. For me, my friends this has nothing to with tradition for I abhor it, but *because Christ was baptized so was I.* And so shall ye if you want to fulfill and reach the fullness of righteous required by the power and authority of the LORD. Amen. It's not about being *dipped in water*, you see how materialistic and carnal your mind is my friend? See it from the eyes of the Spirit brothers and sisters because if you continue like this death will be awaiting you in the afterlife. Heed the words of the Lord friends! *Unless he be born of water and Spirit, he will not enter the Kingdom of God!* Many of you think that just because you have the Holy Ghost you need not to be baptized! That is not so, and very untrue! Have ye not read in the books of Acts, after those who were filled with the Spirit of Christ, then disciples immediately commanded that they be baptized in water(for this was a commandment give by the Lord through His Spirit)! I say this with all confidence to you by the Holy Ghost is not enough to get to heaven my beloved, even though you move by Him, and even though you what you are doing is for Him, know this and see it that your sacrifice and offering to the Lord will be rejected. *Why?* Because you presented Him something that does not equal what He asked for, just like Cain. Cain was trying to do it his own way and present it to God and the LORD rejected his sacrifice, and so will He yours if ye do not what He asks, Amen. Because simply it wasn't what He asked of him.

On the flip side of that neither is being baptized *only in water* will be enough to enter heavens gates, sorry. Come! And be bearers of the Truth, and let Him put His Spirit inside of you and give you power to tread upon scorpions, to endure *tribulation*, to *cast out demons*, to reverse and rebuke curses even sicknesses! Receive the Spirit of the Lord my friends! For where the Spirit of the Lord is there if *freedom*! So be set free from the traditions of men, the rudiments of the world, from the lighting of candles, to carrying statues and worshiping them, to having to wear the long drapes, calling on the name of Mary, and Paul, and call on the Name of Jesus! To be set free some the powers of sin and darkness and overcome with the power and the might of the Light, *Amen*. For there is power in both being baptized in water and by the fire of the Holy Ghost, to bring it forth to you completely here it is. The power of the baptism of water, is the beginning of the process of cleaning from sin then setting you up to receive the power of the Holy Ghost in the manifestation of tongues bringing fire to your spirit, completely burning away desires, wants, lusts, darkness, and any stronghold pertaining to sin. Restoring you back to Image of Christ, of the Father, so that ye may have a chance to enter the Kingdom of God! Now, is this all you have to do after you have received things? Are you finished, are you "*saved*"?

Just because ye have done these things and have allowed the Holy Ghost to fill you, this isn't the end my friends but *only the beginning*! Look at the God of Immediacy, when He went straight to be tested of the evil one, teaching, ministering, healing, prophesying all these things, so I ask of you to not think that you can revert back to sin just because you have *been sealed.* The notion of O.S.A.S., or *once saved always saved* is blasphemy, and is just totally incorrect! Ye think that you cannot lose your salvation after you have been sealed? Just as God grafted out the Israelites, and said that He would graft them back in at the time He has set for them to be, the same is that you can be *grafted out of the vine of salvation because of sin.* For the Lord hath saved you from sin and brought you through the process of refining you by fire, why would ye want to go back(*that is willingly wanting to sin*)? For grace we are saved, and by the Grace of God we shall enter the Kingdom of heaven, of God. Ephesians 2:8-10, *[8] For by grace are ye saved through faith; and that not of yourselves: it is the gift of God: [9]Not of works, lest any man should boast. [10] For we are his workmanship, created in Christ Jesus unto good works, which God hath before ordained that we should walk in them.*

So, my brethren, lay down the notion or the thought of O.S.A.S you see here that you are wrong, or at least were taught wrong my friends.(*And I say all of this humbly.*) Because when you believe this and do this the works of your hands become your *god*, you praise and honor them more than you will honor *God, the One Who created you and the things you worship.* Rest in the Lord this day all men and women, and allow Him to take care of you! For this is what Satan wants and you are falling in his trap my brothers and sisters, that is *worshiping and honoring another god.* Just as the Lord's commandments state. We are only saved by grace and not by the works of our hands, and once we have completed the work that Christ has put in us thence we are *completely* saved, and by His Grace only entering the Kingdom of God. If we follow what the passage states in order to be sealed them we shall stay sealed and redeemed until the day of Redemption comes(*which is not far away, but upon us) when we enter into the gates of God, Amen.*

Going forward, since we have broken the wall and spirit of tradition in Jesus Name, crushing it under our feet by *His Power* just as *He did*, I ask that ye not become traditionalistic *even* in opening yourself up to the *process of salvation*. What I mean by the *process of salvation* is repentance(*contains confession of sin, then leads to accepting the Lord's seed in your heart),* baptism in water(*to fulfill all righteousness to reach the Image of Christ*), being *filled with the power from on High*, by the Holy Ghost with evidence of speaking in tongues, then lastly yet continually in prayer, fasting as needed when the Lord sees fit for you to do so, and most importantly remain in the Word of the Living God, continue to grow in God. Now, with saying that the reason why I say that I hope that you don't become traditionalistic is because, the order and the process leading up to receiving the King's Spirit inside of you is not *specifically* in that order. Personally, I had the grace to go through the steps as listed, yet as the Word of God spoke and clarified that I've seen people filled with the Holy Ghost *then* baptized in the water! It was such a powerful and invigorating moment seeing the Spirit of God move in such a manner, because at that time I've never seen it done nor heard of it! It was beautiful, and what made it even more beautiful was the fact that it lined up so perfectly with the Word of Christ, Amen.

Read this part in Acts with me when this takes place so that you may not *become traditionalistic, nor listen to traditionalism by elders or whomever speaks to you saying it must go in this order. For they are prohibiting the flow of the Spirit of God, because just as the wind comes and blows as it pleases and you know not where it comes from that is how the flow of God is.* He *flows* just as the *wind* and does as He pleases and desires! So I adjure you fellowservants who have the Holy Ghost *do not* prohibit the flow of Christ's Spirit and tamper with what the Lord is trying to do. Amen.

Acts 10:48, *⁴⁸ And he commanded them to be baptized in the name of the Lord(or in the Name of the Lord Jesus Christ for this answers the question for you COGIC believers who baptize **not** in the Name of the Lord Jesus for He is the Father in Heaven, and the One*

Spirit of God whom we have access through to Him by Him, Amen!)Then prayed they him to tarry(or stay with them)certain days.

So it is important to go into the water! No matter what the disciples made sure, even *commanded* as the Word says to be baptized in water *in the Name of the Lord Jesus Christ!* Why? To fulfill all righteousness by God through following the same **exact** footsteps of God in Christ when He came on earth, Amen.

This brings me to my next point, just to clarify *Who's Name* that we should be baptized in when it comes to baptism of water. We are to go out to all nations baptizing in the *name of the Father, and of the Son, and of the Holy Ghost.(Matthew 28:19)* Notice little ones what your Master requires and look at His *Clarification of Himself, and* confirming *Who's Name you should baptize in.* For ye must have the revelation of Christ, understand the mystery of the Servant of God, Who came from God, and Who was indeed the *One True God!* Do you still perceive and not see? Are the thoughts and words of the traditions of your elders swirling in your mind? Teaching you to only baptize in the Name of the Father, and of the Son, and of the Holy Ghost and *not in the Name of Jesus*? Let me tell you my friends, this may come to as a shock to you, and it may even cause many to be angry with me(*yet remember my friends I am only the messenger not the One who gives it, any questions or arguments take it to my King, thank you! For I will not debate the word of Christ with you, only show you the truths in it and maybe that you have missed.*) okay so we see that the Lord Jesus is indeed the Father, the Son, and the Holy Ghost, indeed the Godhead in bodily form(Colossians 2:9-10). Let's again be clear *not three persons in One, not three separate Gods, not two separate Gods, but only One God for in His Word not mine He is called, Wonderful, Counsellor, the mighty God, the Everlasting Father, the Prince of Peace, and indeed the Holy One, yet don't forget Matthew 1:24, he was called Emmanuel meaning, "God with us."* Not *like* God with us, not a *form as in a piece or not fully God(if ye look in scripture He did come in the bodily form of God, that is to say that if God was to come as a human being He would be Jesus and was and still is sitting on the throne of His Glory, Amen and Amen.)* but He *was and is* God, because the Heavenly Father has already declared and proclaimed that there is *NO ONE LIKE HIM*, and *NOR SHALL THERE EVER BE!* So with saying that Christ the Lord Jesus, the Holy One of God could not be *like* God, but He had to *be God* in the fullness in His form or else our God would be a liar and His Word wouldn't be true! See Isaiah 46:9, *⁹ Remember the former things of old: for I am God, and there is none else; I am God, and there is none like Me.*

He says this many, many, many, many, many, many times my friends do you not yet see? I ask that if you do not still please take into consideration what the Lord has said through me here in chapter two and one I adjure you pray over the knowledge that was *given* and look for a flaw *along with the Word of God* and tell me if I lie. But if you don't go by the word of God and only by your conscience and what you've learned your rebuttal will and shall be null and void to me. For yes, I shall listen but it won't matter because ye did not go strictly by the Word of God, Amen.

Isaiah 45:21-22, *²¹ Tell ye, and bring them near; yea, let them take counsel together: who hath declared this from ancient time? who hath told it from that time?* **have not I the LORD? and there is no God else beside me; a just God and a Saviour; there is none beside me.**

²² Look unto me, and be ye saved, all the ends of the earth: for I am God, and there is none else.

Is my God a liar? Is He a man that He should repent? Does He deceive and manipulate? No! For that is the darkness and the way of Satan!! He has lied to you! God is not a man that he shall lie, nor is He a son of man that He should repent! Who would He repent to? *He is God and there is none else, neither is there any beside Him(trinitarians), neither is there any one like Him!* I pray that you see the Word of Christ and His Authorship and His Oneness for there is none else like Him!! So when He came and claimed the Title as Savior, you scholars should have understood that that was and is the *same God from the Old Testament!* For nothing came through, nothing exists without Christ Jesus for He is the author of His Word! It is *inspired, or breathed out through His servants by Him! There is **none else!*** Be ye set free from the hold of Satan! For he loves to deceive and manipulate you, and cause you to worship a false god for that is something that the Lord God abhors the most! So what do you think that he will do? Satan is cunning and crafty beware the yeast of the Pharisees, for it may seem good and well-pleasing but I adjure you not to take from them for that one measure will bring upon death, and corruption, and heavy burdens upon you and the wrath of Christ! But the yeast of the bread of Life will indeed be sufficient enough to carry you hither and thence, Amen!

Do ye remember the warning? Do ye remember the words of the Holy Ghost spoken through by one of the apostles, Apostle Paul in 1 Timothy 4:1-6,

[1] Now the Spirit speaketh expressly, that in the latter times some shall depart from the faith, giving heed to seducing spirits, and doctrines of devils;

[2] Speaking lies in hypocrisy; having their conscience seared with a hot iron;

[3] Forbidding to marry, and commanding to abstain from meats, which God hath created to be received with thanksgiving of them which believe and know the truth.

[4] For every creature of God is good, and nothing to be refused, if it be received with thanksgiving:

[5] For it is sanctified by the word of God and prayer.

[6] If thou put the brethren in remembrance of these things, thou shalt be a good minister of Jesus Christ, nourished up in the words of faith and of good doctrine, whereunto thou hast attained.

For what I am about to say, I say by the unction of the Holy Ghost in fear and trembling, humbly in no fear of the word of man, nor their blasphemy, and slander against me. But before ye start plotting and scheming against, wanting to prohibit me from where the Lord God is taking me, trying to *sabotage*, first think to yourself, *Is this the way of God?* Save yourself the trouble for if I am wrong in any of the words that *He* has told me to speak, He shall strike me down, and I shall be condemned. But I wish to be a good minister, a righteous servant of *the Lord Jesus Christ*, and I wish to do all things out of love by the Spirit of Love inside of me. For if I did love thee this book wouldn't have been published for you.

So without further a due I will say this to you trinitarians first that your doctrine has been created by *devils*, by the crafty hands of Satan! Woe, unto those who helped orchestrate this, and those who have followed *blindly* in their steps. Because ye believe to do everything in Jesus Name except for baptism, did the Lord God say do *everything in His Name*? Including baptism?(*Matthew 28:19*) Also look at this, look at how cunning Satan is my friends, he whispered into the ears of your forefathers, and those who are "*above*" you now, "Surely God didn't say to baptize in Jesus Name, but look at what He *did* say to baptize in the Name of the Father, and of the Son, and of the Holy Ghost? You gotta follow the Word and *Only* what *He says* right?" The devil birthed this forth to trap you my friends! For the Lord the Creator of His Own Doctrine and Word, speaks against your belief! Colossians 3:17, *17 And whatsoever ye do in word or deed, do all in the name of the Lord Jesus, giving thanks to God and the Father by him.* So how can you forbid the Word of God and what He saith for you to do? Who are you to do so? Who were your forefathers, the creators and schemors of this doctrine that they willingly defy the word of God and condemn many others with their traditions? There were created from the dusts of this world and so *did they return, Amen.* But the Lord God died, and rose again by His *Own Power*, so why do ye worship your leaders, and the works of their hands? When the Lord God *shewed greats things before, when there were no strange gods among you.*

You may be asking, *How did Satan deceive me*? *How are we in the wrong?* Perceive and see my brother and sisters for the Lord God shall show you in word, by what *He* has *given* me. For lo, *the Lord God Almighty Jesus*, the Christ said to be baptized in His Name for ye shall be cleansed and receive *power from on High from the Father. Once you are baptized in the Name of the Lord you are indeed embedded in Him and no man or devil in hell shall pluck you out of His Hand, neither the Father's Hand, and you become in His Ownership.* And the devil knows this so what does he do? He causes confusion among you to not baptize in the Name of the Father, and of the Son, and of the Holy Ghost in Jesus Christ's Mighty Name(*that is in Jesus Mighty Name) so that you will never become one of His and remain carnal, and one of his.* Do everything else, *but* baptize in the Name of Jesus, one of the most pinnacle pieces of salvation you leave His Name out? DO YOU NOT SEE THE DECEPTION HERE? SATAN IS AS A LION SEEKING WHOM he MAY DEVOUR! Ye are his dinner and have been caught by his claw(*traditions of your elders, legalism, systemic religions pulling you further and further from the Father when He has already been in reach for you yet you depend on yourself to free yourself by His Power! You see not His Hand out to you but look at the traditions, rather your elders to pull you out, yet they are over in there high chairs and cannot hear thee.*) and be consumed by his corruption and manipulation! Get out before it's too late! For here is the Lord again through me reaching out to you offering you truth and salvation once again, *call on Him while He is yet near*!

If ye are not born of the water in the name of the Lord, and were baptized in the Name of the Father, and of the Son, and of the Holy(*saying this when you are baptized and not the name of Jesus*) who spirit did ye receive? And what spirit did ye move by? For there are imitating and similar spirits, counterfeits, antichrist spirits who have their language, also there is witch tongue beware this as well for the witches will try to blend in! Perceive and see them point them out *by the Spirit of God as He leads not when you feel to do so, Amen.* For the Name of the Father is Jesus Christ, for the Name of the Son is Jesus Christ, and the Name of the Holy Ghost is Jesus Christ so in what name did ye enter? Of what father, of what son, of what *"holy"* ghost? For there is *One name under heaven(which is exalted above **every name**, see Philippians 2:9-11) whence men must be saved by and that is the powerful Name of the Lord Jesus Christ!* Acts 4:10-12,

[10] Be it known unto you all, and to all the people of Israel, that by the name of Jesus Christ of Nazareth, whom ye crucified, whom God raised from the dead, even by him doth this man stand here before you whole.
[11] This is the stone which was set at nought of you builders, which is become the head of the corner.
[12] Neither is there salvation in any other: for there is none other name under heaven given among men, whereby we must be saved.

So with saying that my friends you cannot be saved in the Name of the Father without being baptized in the Name of Jesus Christ for He is the Father, you cannot with the Son, and you cannot with the Holy Ghost for *He is the Holy Ghost!* Acts 20:28, *²⁸ Take heed therefore unto yourselves, and to all the flock, over the which **the Holy Ghost** hath made you overseers, to feed the church of God, which **he hath purchased with his own blood**.* I ask of you that you will pray on these things so that you can be saved *for real*, and be baptized in the *Name of Jesus, the Lord of Grace* for His Arms are open to you now despite of what you have done, what spiritual crimes you hath committed, what sacrilege you have done, His heart still burns for you with Love and wishes for you not to perish for lack of knowledge especially when it is presented right before your eyes! For there are wolves among you who wish not to spare you but to devour your soul and bring you along with them to place they call home(*that is hell*) for the seducing spirits have a great hold upon them and the *same spirits* wish to grab a hold of you (*Beware my friends*). *Know* this scripture and bare this in your heart for these days, especially, so that ye may keep watch(*in the Spirit as well as the physical*).

*Acts 20:29-31, ²⁹ For I know this, that after my departing **shall**(this was promised to their generation and ours my friends so keep watch for these wolves so that they may not enter the herd of sheep among us!) grievous wolves enter in among you, not sparing the flock. ³⁰ Also of your own selves shall men arise, speaking perverse things, to **draw away disciples** after them.*
³¹ Therefore watch, and remember, that by the space of three years I ceased not to warn every one night and day with tears.

These wolves have entered, made an abode in the churches, set up camp, and are deceiving as they please and we with the power to stop are doing nothing. I come in the name of the Lord with power and by the Grace of the Lord to uproot your seats in the church and send you back to depths *whence you came from,* and restore what you have destroyed, and destroy what ye have built! For no longer will you chase and burden the Sheep of God, for the Lord shall smite thee with His Mighty Rod and Staff and send thee back to hell where you belong for your power and time has run out, I *by the Holy Ghost of Christ* am putting you on notice, on foreclosure! Get it right with the Lord turn from your wicked ways, for if you do not want what you do behind closed doors to be exposed by the Lord I adjure you take this step. Step down from your "*high place*" that you have built for yourself and humble yourselves before the Lord of Hosts thy God and do not test Him. For if ye tempt the Lord of Hosts and His Mighty Power to expose, and chastise get ready for a change of things. For you have been put on notice those of you among the flock, you goats, and wolves in sheep's clothing, ye hypocrites! You vipers! Awaiting the attack on the flock, by the power that has been given from the Lord unto me I dispose of your plan! For it has been cancelled, denied, revoked, foreclosed, done away with, uprooted in Jesus Mighty Name! *Lord confound their language that they may not go through with their plans and schemes to destroy your people! For whence they come out to destroy me, for they shall come, have Your Hand right there covering me, and let your Blood cover my family in Your Mighty Name, Heavenly Father, Amen and Amen!*

Receive ye the power and be filled with the fullness that is in Christ to heal, to teach, to heal, to minister, to prophecy, to cast out demons, and to be able to perceive and see for the Holy Ghost will help you with these things! For He has given much and will continue to give and reveal more to you by His Spirit(*or by Him, by His Way Amen!*), for many gifts for me has He given and only by Him can you work *in these gifts(I adjure please read, Ephesians 4:9-16)*. Also, remember little sheep, not to become traditionalistic, legalistic, neither systemic in *even doing the things which are right so that ye may not prohibit the work the Spirit of the Holy One. But given Him clear way and access to do what He must to restore you and all men, Amen! Let Him have His Way! Praise the God of Heaven for He is good in the morning, all the way until the night when everyone is asleep! For even my soul praises you O King, for thou art Mighty and shall be praised, worshiped, highly exalted, loved and adored for ever and ever, and You shall reign for ever and ever, Selah. Amen and Amen, Shout Hallelujah to the King of Glory with a great shout! Amen!*

3. Only by Faith can ye endure

What is Faith? And why do we need it? What is the substance of it? *For faith is the substance of things hoped for, the evidence of things not seen (by the naked eye, Hebrews 11:1).* For faith has a very important role in this *Christ-walk* for by faith did Abraham *follow God* and did what He asked, bringing all his descendants(*that is both physical descendants and those of us who are a part of his descendants through the Spirit of God, receiving the promise of the Spirit of Christ in us as Gentiles, Amen!*) across the earth. Let us go to scripture to understand the power of faith, and what it can do.

Let's start at one of the most famous scriptures that Jesus spoke concerning the power of *faith. Matthew 17:20,* [20] *And Jesus said unto them,* "*Because of your unbelief: for verily I say unto you, If ye have faith as a grain of mustard seed, ye shall say unto this mountain, Remove hence to yonder place; and it shall remove; and nothing shall be impossible unto you.*" For this is a very powerful statement my friends, very powerful indeed! Think not in your carnal mind, "*The mountain cannot really be moved from its foundation, can it?*" Why do ye doubt? Why deny the power of God? Be not of the Pharisees but of Jesus who had immense faith in the Father to do mighty acts in front of the eyes that He chose! God created these things and has given man dominion over earth(*look in Genesis when the LORD speaks to Adam for the first time)* yet being obedient to *Him,* t*he King.* Why couldn't we with the faith in God *say to this mountain, Remove hence to yonder place and it shall move*? Your carnal mind which is of the devil will automatically deny and reject such truths, yet I ask you to deny yourself(*Matthew 16:24),* humble yourselves before the Lord and I promise that you will see the power of God like never before(*James 4:10)*!

We cannot put our Lord God in a box, I do not want a God that can be detained! I want a radical God Who willingly wants to show His power and do when He pleases! For *He knows* what He is doing, why would I make a rebuttal *against Him*? Come my friends for now ye know that the power from on High requires faith to receive, and by faith shall ye do the works of God my friends! For *nothing shall be impossible unto you*.

When the devil saw that the Lord God was giving us a chance to receive such power from heaven by access through the faith in the Lord Jesus, he immediately went to work. Why do you think that he *caused* men to create other doctrines and traditionalistic practices? To stop the flow and the power of God my friends, because structure created by men was and is to be destroyed by the LORD for our structure is corrupt and not of the Lord because He doesn't go by the law of man, but by *His Law* which is more suitable for us. For His *Ways and His thoughts are higher and greater than ours*, so unless He allows we could never know the mind of God or why He does certain things(*so just have faith!)*. As a carnal man, who loves structure and control over things this may give you anxiety, but hearken unto me for this *Man, this God, who came as a Mighty Man*, is not a Man that He should lie nor repent for He is holy and just, and is Worthy to take care of you! Forget structure and traditionalism, for His Way is better, and this is also another *prohibited*, if you will, by the devil to try use to prohibit the flow and the move of our Holy God! Be not used by Satan to prohibit God's will and work for your end shall be shameful, move or you will be move my friends!

Give God glory for His Power is not of this world, but of His Own. And He being Graceful and Loving is willing to distribute this power through faith in Him! *For with God nothing is impossible!* Have faith in God! Trust and only believe in the One True God who came and willingly died for your sins so that you may **not** be condemned to an eternal hell which is the *total separation from Him!*

Our God moves where there's faith, or else if there is no faith it displeases Him and He isn't able to work due to the fact that no one has the faith for Him to do what He wants to do for you, not that He can't but wont for He is a Gentleman and doesn't come or go or even do anything if He is not welcomed to(*look at the state of America and all the things that are taking place* **because** *we pushed Him out of schools taking out the very thing that was protecting us, prayer and it will only get worse! So don't blame God for the mass shootings if you want to blame someone* **blame the government, the school boards, and all the parents who decided it'd be best to take this action**. *And because of that brutish act, look at how the little children suffer!).* Let's take a look at Jesus in His Ministry and how the *lack of faith* prohibited the healing and miracles He wanted to do.

Let's take a look at *Mark 6:1-6, ¹And he went out from thence, and came into his own country; and his disciples follow him.*

² And when the sabbath day was come, he began to teach in the synagogue: and many hearing him were astonished, saying, From whence hath this man these things? and what wisdom is this which is given unto him, that even such mighty works are wrought by his hands?

³ Is not this the carpenter, the son of Mary, the brother of James, and Joses, and of Juda, and Simon? and are not his sisters here with us? And they were offended at him.

⁴ But Jesus, said unto them, "A prophet is not without honour, but in his own country, and among his own kin, and in his own house."

⁵ And he could there do no mighty work, save that he laid his hands upon a few sick folk, and healed them.

⁶ And he marvelled because of their unbelief. And he went round about the villages, teaching.

Look at this friends, among His own people whence *He came from and grew up with Him*, were still blinded and knew Him not. They were *offended* of Him, and went off the physical appearance, thinking Him to a common man, rather than the King that He was. Because of their unbelief, and rather concerned where He learned His teaching from being carnal and materialistic as in *Who He was* rather than the help that He was giving for those that were sick! They didn't want Him doing those things, and yes were *offended* of Him because they knew not whence He came it lowered their faith in Him, God to do the works that were needed. So we see without faith it put a slowing down to the work and the flow of God!

If a man is sent to you speaking things of wisdom, teaching and ministering with power, healing and grace given by the LORD Whom ye believe in, even though you knew him to be someone that lived by you and you grew up with him would you pray with him and have faith in the LORD with him or would your common knowledge of him prohibit your faith in the God that is working through Him? Have faith in God my friends! We wanna see God pull people out of wheelchairs, and bring the dead back to life, set free the captives, cast out demons, but your lack of faith is prohibiting the move of God for Him to do so! Do ye not remember the works of Jesus the Christ? He healed the blind men, paralytics, cured those with the palsy, *maimed to be whole*. Do ye not think that our God can do such things today? Yes He can and only by faith can we see and do these things my friends, think not a person who is among you cannot move in the anointing of God. Be not *prohibitory*, but a *believer in Christ my friends*.

The scriptures will be fulfilled though *that a prophet is not without honour, but in his own country, and among his own kin, among his own house*. No matter who you are, just because your family those that know you will think of you to be common, someone that cannot rise above and do such things. And because of their common knowledge of who you are they'll ask prohibiting the move of God, "Where did he learn these things? Where was he taught?" Out of indignation, and like I said common knowledge of you. So prophets! Be not dismayed nor angered when you family, or *kin* doesn't respond well to the words of the Lord that you bring to their ears, or when you ask to pray and God heals them and instead of saying, "*Thank you, Jesus!*" They bombard you with all kinds of questions!

Faith can truly move mountains whether they be physical or spiritual mountains my friends. For God's strength is not measured by what men think or can comprehend! We must believe in the only God that there is and the *same that descended to fill all things, and show us the works that are possible*. Think not that you can achieve these things on your own my friends, but with God all things are possible! His Power is immeasurable and is willing to bestow it upon all flesh, but the *lack of faith is prohibiting the access of His Power to do so!* We pray for miracles for our loved ones, for the mothers in the church, for those who are in wheelchairs, those who have been in the hospital to come out and be free from sickness, yet we don't have the faith for it to happen and it when it does you doubt. Why? Our God is not limited! Break free from the mind of carnality and be in the mind of the Spirit of the Lord knowing that all things are possible and that nothing will be impossible to you because of your Faith in the Holy King!

The Holy One spoke unto me this morning and said unto me this beautiful thing, "*I don't move off of money from men, or what you can give Me. Rather I move off of Faith, Faith is the currency of heaven, and so is righteousness.*" *saith the LORD of Hosts and Mercy.* For He had the foreknowledge that I would be writing this and gave me this prayer! Isn't He good? He loves to make sure that we are prepared for what He called us to do! Anyhow, just to break this down into terms for those of you who don't understand. This is how I saw it and the LORD approved of it, think of a sales clerk he won't move unless the *money* is given unto him to check out. *Money* is the currency of man, is what gets a men to do anything for you, but when it pertains to God your money is useless, but faith...now faith is something that He moves in and if it be His Will anything that you ask for in His Name in Faith He will do it for you, *Amen!* Now you may ask, Why do does God ask us to sow into ministries then? Why does He love a cheerful giver if our money absolutely means nothing to Him? To help you understand and comprehend the money, the paper money, check whatever you use to sow, yes that means nothing for it is in the part *of giving something that is of high value to you* is the part that matters. A *cheerful giver* is not just in money as some greedy pastors and bishops use the scripture to make it see that way *because* they are so *materialistic* and want to profit from the gospel. Rather it is more than that giving food to a homeless person when you have none, giving your last dime not unto man, but unto the Lord of Hosts, but just like wolves they use different tactics to bate you to sowing not into the ministry of God rather be *sowers of and into their pockets.*

Look at the woman who Jesus *honors* in the Gospels who gave all she had in *Mark 12:41-44*, *41 And Jesus sat over against the treasury, and beheld how the people cast money into the treasury: and many that were rich cast in much.*

42 And there came a certain poor widow, and she threw in two mites, which make a farthing.

43 And he called unto him his disciples, and saith unto them, "*Verily I say unto you, That this poor widow hath cast more in, than all they which have cast into the treasury:*

44 For all they did cast in of their abundance; but she of her want did cast in all that she had, even all her living."

God sees the heart of the giver, for she did this is faith, giving her all. If you had the last twenty dollars in your pocket would you willingly with a *cheerful heart in faith* give it to God? Or would you say, "This is all I have LORD." in doubt thinking that He cannot make a way? I have a testimony, for I am a witness of giving unto the Lord as in to a particular ministry. I went one year to a conference, and I had some money for food, and things to buy for myself. Each and every time they called for an offering I put one in giving it to the Lord with faith to bless the ministry even though I didn't have much to begin with. And just when I thought I had no more money God made sure that I never ran out. Every time I looked around someone was giving me money in my hand! My relatives, people who wanted to be kind, it was amazing to see what God does when you are obedient to Him. I didn't do this just so I could, but to be a blessing while my time was there in the conference and the Lord God of Peace and Grace blessed me during my travels with favor, and money in my pocket, Amen.

So give not because you have money in abundance for the Lord looks not at those offerings, but even though *when* you have and you give cheerfully as if you are giving your last that pleases Him! And those of you who don't have yet give your all with your heart and with faith trust me I guarantee you, the Lord God will not leave you penniless or without the things you need, Amen.

One thing I want to say is that we must have faith in each other's anointings that God has placed in each and everyone of us. Have faith in

God that He can do what He has called your brother or sister to do, pray for them keep them lifted up with all love and supplication helping them if God permits, but I adjure you *beware the spirit of jealousy* for it creeps upon you and before you know it you'll be acting out on it trying to be *in the way of God*, becoming a stumblingblock for your fellow brothers and sisters. I ask that you stay focused and remember this that if one gains we all gain, if one is wounded we all suffer along with the one that is wounded. If ye rejoice in another's misery are ye of the Lord's? Is your heart in the right place? Give no room to the enemy my friends for each of us has different anointings upon our lives, some are meant for local ministries, some city wide, some state wide, some country wide, some world wide, but know and understand that **no one** and I mean **no one** is above nor better than anyone else! You may have traveled the world and ministered but once you were a sinner like me, and vice versa my friends for we all need each other. Jealousy is such an ugly demon, why is it in the church today? Because we have become so materialistic, carnal, and judgemental that all we look at now is the physical appearance of a man or woman rather than in the spirit. One person could *seem* have it all together like the Pharisees yet be dead inside and know not what they preach, and someone that may not have the nice clothes wear the high heels like you *ladies* yet be full of the Holy Ghost and has the anointing to reign fire from heaven. Stop judging and putting labels on people! For God is the only Judge for He is Holy and Just who are you? No one to judge that is who you are.

Moving forward in the topic of faith. Faith is such a powerful tool to have especially in the times that we are in now, *the end times.* For only by faith can ye endure this Christ-walk with its trials and tribulations and only by faith can ye endure the times that are written in the word that *are here.* I perceive in the Spirit that many of you know not that we will endure persecution and have believed the great lie and deception that has come through the mouths of your pastors and elders. Do ye not remember the words of Jesus, my friends? Look to John 15:18-21,

> [18] *If the world hate you, ye know that it hated me before it hated you.*

19 If ye were of the world, the world would love his own: but because ye are not of the world, but I have chosen you out of the world, therefore the world hateth you.

20 Remember the word that I said unto you, The servant is not greater than his lord. If they have persecuted me, they will also persecute you; if they have kept my saying, they will keep yours also.

21 But all these things will they do unto you for my name's sake, because they know not him that sent me.

You cannot deny this scripture *no longer* my friends for this is very straight for and prayerful easy to comprehend, think not that the Savior of this world came and was persecuted for the faith that He created for you and you not endure the same? They knew not His Father and he who hates the Son hates the Father also because they are indeed One, and their Name is Christ Jesus! This is why the Comforter being inside of you is so important for He shall *comfort and counsel* you through these perilous times, why are ye afraid? Your pastors who told you that you will not endure for the faith and that we will be received unto Christ before those times is flat out lying to you! For they will now say things unto to just to keep you in church, and to say things that are easy for you to receive so that they can continue to get a revenue every week from your money. Think not that my friends that you aren't going to endure because the disciples did, the LORD GOD as a man did and so will you who are to escape, and think that you will overcome without *overcoming?* Have you searched the scriptures my friends, or do you just believe in pastor, bishop, or teacher so much that you don't test the spirits regardless to what they say? Or was it that when they told you this that it felt good that you weren't going to be persecuted and you knew that when you went to scriptures that you'd find the truth? This is another case of following the traditions of men, and the rudiments of this world and ***not after Christ and His Word!*** This angers me righteously my friends because we have allowed this lie to sweep through the Church as those of you who know the truth are too afraid to speak the truth! Come on saints! Have faith in the One who created the individuals who have lied and if they lay a hand on you or try trust in the Lord that He will protect you and keep you.

If I didn't trust God enough, I wouldn't be writing this book from the Lord unto to you but I fear no man! I only fear the One who can kill my flesh and destroy it in hell. Your weapons are carnal, but *His are of the heavens which I fear the most.* God has said and I will write it again so that you can see,

¹⁸ If the world hate you, ye know that it hated me before it hated you.

¹⁹ If ye were of the world, the world would love his own: but because ye are not of the world, but I have chosen you out of the world, therefore the world hateth you.

²⁰ Remember the word that I said unto you, The servant is not greater than his lord. If they have persecuted me, they will also persecute you; if they have kept my saying, they will keep yours also.

²¹ But all these things will they do unto you for my name's sake, because they know not him that sent me.

Your fear of this world and its "power" causes you to crack under pressure and you sit in a corner faithless and unbelieving in the God of Power, do ye not know the story of Noah? And how the God of creation carried Him in the ark as He destroyed those who were full of sin? Do you not know that the same God who stopped the waves from killing His Disciples is the *same One* from the beginning? He will protect you and has given you knowledge of the *power from on High, and the faith that is required to endure* such times that are upon us. But you have been blinded by your fellowservants who know not of what they speak or the truth about what they were taught, from your pastors and elders who have no oil to teach what is right so they tell you what you want to hear. Wanting the glory from you rather than deny himself and hearken unto the voice of the Holy One and telling you what is right! Listen my friends this is not easy to tell you but *the love* that I have for you from the Lord far outweighs my concerns or worries of what your rebuttal will be let's look to *another* scripture to clarify and so that you may step into the truth that is found in the word of Christ!

First I would like for you to see the that the times that we are in are the *perilous time* that the Lord speaks of, 2 Timothy 3:1-9,

¹ This know also, that in the last days perilous times shall come.

² For men shall be lovers of their own selves, covetous, boasters, proud, blasphemers, disobedient to parents, unthankful, unholy,

³ Without natural affection, trucebreakers, false accusers, incontinent, fierce, despisers of those that are good,

⁴ Traitors, heady, highminded, lovers of pleasures more than lovers of God;

⁵ Having a form of godliness, but denying the power thereof: from such turn away.

⁶ For of this sort are they which creep into houses, and lead captive silly women laden with sins, led away with divers lusts,

⁷ Ever learning, and never able to come to the knowledge of the truth.

⁸ Now as Jannes and Jambres withstood Moses, so do these also resist the truth: men of corrupt minds, reprobate concerning the faith.

⁹ But they shall proceed no further: for their folly shall be manifest unto all men, as theirs also was.

Lo, and behold all these that are listed before you are happening now. We see many people being lovers of themselves both in the church and in the world, as in the world this will always happen, but when ye see the elders and those of your fellowservants turning cold and uplifting themselves more than they uplift God this is a problem! That is why it is listed to warn you. For there are covetors among the brethren whom wish to destroy those who quote on quote *are becoming better* than them and desire their household rather than being grateful for what God has given them! For you see next the *boasters*, there are many of them that are proud and haughty in the Church today my friends and one thing that the Lord is showing me now is it has to do with the titles that men give themselves(as in prophets when they really want to *profit*, preachers that preach for money as if this work that we do for Christ is valued by money, apostles who are leading people to hell with traditions and heavy laden burdens, evangelists who *evangelize* their name more than they *evangelize* the name and the Gospel of Jesus Christ, teachers who teach with evil doctrines that only consist of prosperity and wealth without the

King) uplifting their brand when they have been branded by Christ. Letting the world know of how they became prosperous doing this and that without ever giving enough thanks to the One Who gave them those things. Proud pastors and worship leaders who belittle everyone because who they know that are famous, proud in *their own accomplishments.* You can very easily boast in the title that you gave yourself, but when God has called you to a specific work you need not to declare who you are *title wise* let the work speak for itself my friends and never forget that the power and the grace you have to preach doesn't come from you, but from *the King of Power, Jesus Christ only.* God has given us a list as to what the state of the Church and the world would be in to signify that *this is the end.* Do ye not see and perceive the foreknowledge and the love that God gives us? Our God is the only One who knows the day and the time of His coming, but Him being such a beautiful Spirited man is willing to let us even know the events leading up to this. *Hallelujah! Thanks, honor, and glory belongs to you my King Jehovah!* Study the list of things that concern the perilous times my friends and perceive and see through the Spirit as you go through the day and see as these things have *already begun*, and they will so ever increase as the days get *darker and darker* my friends.

Now that we understand and see the times are upon us and already working we can now go and see more of the *events that will surely take place before the return of our Lord and Savior, Christ Jesus!* Let's read and break down together the scripture 2 Thessalonians 2:1-12,

¹Now we beseech you, brethren, by the coming of our Lord Jesus Christ, and by our gathering together unto him,

² That ye be not soon shaken in mind, or be troubled, neither by spirit, nor by word, nor by letter as from us, as that the day of Christ is at hand.

³ Let no man deceive you by any means: for that day shall not come, except there come a falling away first, and that man of sin be revealed, the son of perdition;

⁴ Who opposeth and exalteth himself above all that is called God, or that is worshipped; so that he as God sitteth in the temple of God, shewing himself that he is God.

⁵ Remember ye not, that, when I was yet with you, I told you these things?

⁶ And now ye know what withholdeth that he might be revealed in his time.

⁷ For the mystery of iniquity doth already work: only he who now letteth will let, until he be taken out of the way.

⁸ And then shall that Wicked be revealed, whom the Lord shall consume with the spirit of his mouth, and shall destroy with the brightness of his coming:

⁹ Even him, whose coming is after the working of Satan with all power and signs and lying wonders,

¹⁰ And with all deceivableness of unrighteousness in them that perish; because they received not the love of the truth, that they might be saved.

¹¹ And for this cause God shall send them strong delusion, that they should believe a lie:

¹² That they all might be damned who believed not the truth, but had pleasure in unrighteousness.

Many people have a hard time understanding this scripture, more so they have chosen to believe the lie of pre-tribulation rapture that any truths that come their way they still deny it, for they are so set on this lie. Understand and know that is so much easier swallowing a lie rather than swallowing the pill of truth which is the post-tribulation. We see that is the Paul is clearly talking about the gathering of the saints is the air with the Lord, or the *catching away with Christ.* Then following that so that you don't be afraid, nor shaken in mind or spirit, by word or letter, *because we as the saints of God aren't appointed to wrath(1 Thessalonians 5:9), only to endure persecution for the day of Christ is at hand.* But so that no man deceive you, in word, letter, presentation that this day will not come to pass unless there be a *great falling away.* So we see clearly that Paul is indeed discussing *the day of Christ* when He returns in glory to receive His people, and with saying that this will *not take place until the man of sin(or the main antichrist, the devil, himself) is revealed.* We will be here in that time my friends don't you see? Why else would Paul being lead by the Holy Ghost go into such detail if it had nothing to do with us? The True believers in Christ? I adjure you to look my friends, *study with the Holy Ghost*, and not your spirit for that is where false doctrines arise. Your fear creates things that aren't so, and in this day and age that we are in do you not see the signs?

The belief of us *escaping* persecution is contrary to the word in many different ways friends, because when those of you who believe this you think, "The Lord Christ loves me why would He want me to endure this, therefore this doctrine cannot be true!" But listen unto me my friends for the voice which I listen to is the same One that spoke to the disciples back in their day, the whole church has believed this lie. Look at the state of the church! We're mixing the ways of God with the ways of the world(or of Satan), saying that you can live this way and still be saved, that there is *no hell,* the church itself is speaking blasphemous things that are contrary to the Redemptive work of Christ and the Word of God. And no one stands up and says anything. *By the way those of you who believe the lie that the church is telling, believing that there is no hell, those of you who straightly deny the word of Christ, and the power and authority of God you are indeed apart of the forming Apostasy Church.* Whose doctrine is straightly against the Word of God, who Christ was and is, the time of His coming, anything contrary to the Spirit of God or His way is that of the antichrist which is running rampant! Satan is coming and will unleash hell like never before on this earth. Those who don't bow to him and his image, take his mark will either face death or bend to his will. Sadly, many of you will bend and crack just to save your own life, for you did not get the oil while the oil was being pressed out friends! For you who speak and "preach' in the churches(*not all, but a mass majority)* of you have no power in the Holy Ghost and the *moving of the Holy Ghost* as you call it is a hoax. And you are deceiving many, but know this your day is coming if you don't repent the wrath of the Lord will devour you on that *terrible day.*

There have been many biblical events that have happened over these last few months(*depending on when you read this)* Israel celebrating it's seventieth birthday, them joining the America Embassy, whence I first saw the news of the American Embassy joining or having *any part* of them the first thing that dropped in my Spirit was *the trodden of the Gentiles.* And I felt that we were seeing the beginning sign of this, so beware for somewhere is this Satan will arise claiming to be God, the Christ. *When ye see the armies surrounding Jerusalem, those of you in Judea flee to the mountains, those of you who are on the rooftops come down not to get any clothes but flee, and I say flee to the mountains. For this will be one of the signs of the abomination of desolation, or Satan.* And with all the hatred and envy coming against Israel from Iran, Pakistan, the formations that are arising claiming that they side with those opposing Israel, we see these things slowly but surely happening friends do ye not see? Please, please, please put down all that you think you know and listen to the Lord and have faith in for only be faith can ye endure these things! Verily, verily, I say unto you friends once again many of you will turn from the faith in fear of persecution and the coming events, but *blessed is those who endure to the end,* **saith the Lord of Power and Grace.**

Back to those who believe this I say unto you again it is contrary to the word of God, and what sad is that many of those who believe this doctrine have not ye the *Holy Ghost* nor believe in Him. Nor do you understand the Oneness of God, yet you think that you will be *caught away with God.* For God has shown me much concerning this and the spiritual predicament that you are in, and you are still at the beginning stages of the faith! Think on these things believers of this doctrine, my friends, you try to put a date on the coming of Christ when He specifically told you that no one knows but the Father, so when you say to people, *"I have a date for when the Lord God returns!"* You greatly do err! For are you the Father? Do you sit on the right hand of God? Are you in power? Where were they when the King of Israel laid the foundations of the earth? I can tell you, *you were nowhere to be found!* For only the Father knows! And the Hand of the Lord is against you when you utter such blasphemies, why do you say such things? I can surely by the Holy Ghost tell you the answer. Because you see the events that you know to be true are unfolding and because of your fear of persecution you began to try to find something to prove that doctrine, to feed the lie. As my mom wisely taught me by the Holy Ghost that you cannot feed a lie with another lie, for it will surely fall through! I bring a rebuke to you! God is not pleased with you for the things that you have done to try to prove that false doctrine of you escaping persecution has caused you to do a great crime against the littles ones, and God is not a God that lets you get away with such doings!

Look at the heartbreak, terror, division, hopelessness and mockery that you bring against the Gospel of Christ when you do such things. It waters down the words of Christ and what He said about His return for you say, "I know the day!" Then He doesn't come, that should wake you up! Yet you go back confused, not understanding why it is that He didn't come? Because the doctrine you believe is *FALSE!* For you know nothing of His coming! He gave us clear instruction, a flat out guide telling us of what would take place before His return but as I said because your flesh is weak and you listen not to the Spirit of God you believe what is easier and *what makes sense to you.* All of the disciples died for the faith, yet are living in Christ in the life that we have not seen yet. Why do you fear the creation and not the Creator? You twist up His doctrine to fit yours to please man yet not listen to what He has to say. I am His mouthpiece and I say unto you His Words so those of you that do these things will see that you are greatly wrong and in great error. For this is what the LORD of Hosts says unto you those of you who believe the false doctrine and are spreading false truths, *" My Hand is against you, My eye is upon you for I have seen the great pain that you have caused those new to the faith and the confusion that you have caused to the old. The outrage that you have brought forth with your false doctrines. For if ye not repent and heed to the words of My servant you will surely perish, for his Words are not his own but of Me, your Lord and Savior, the King of kings, and the Lord of lords, the Messiah, the God who came upon the earth declared and healed, the one who justly walked upright as the Son of God, the One Who rose again for you, your Holy One and Redeemer. Hearken unto My voice, for blessed are those who hear My voice through his, and blessed are those who see my Word in his for I have chosen Him, Amen."* saith *the Lord of All Power, Strength, and Grace, Amen!*

For I not bare record of myself, for I am His servant not my own servant, for I did not send myself to declare my own gospel, but the Gospel of the One Who saved me from death and a burning hell, *Amen.* The Lord is pleased with those who hear, and with those who see what He says for only the true sheep heareth the voice of his Shepherd, but the goats who are of another shepherd hear not His Voice nor knoweth the Father of our Shepherd. *I thank God for those of you who hear the voice of the Lord speaking to you. Holy Father for You are clothed in Majesty, Glory and Power and I give You will give You glory, glory, glory, and honor all honor to You forever and ever! For Great is Thy Faithfulness and wonderful are Your thoughts towards me for you love with a great Love that I cannot measure with a ruler, for there is no number that is of a great enough value to equate the value of Your Love, O LORD. Amen and Amen. I bless You O Mighty God, for my Hallelujah and thanks belong to You and Your Great and Powerful Name! Thank You Jesus, O Mighty Savior and King! Selah!*

Strong faith is required for this journey friends! I hope that by this point that ye understand the move of God and what He is about the do, the wrath that He is bringing upon the earth and I hope that ye are not in the way of wrath but are clothed in His Truth that it may provide protection like no other from the horrible tragedies and calamities that are ahead. Keep the oil in your lamps fellowservants give not to the other virgins, those of you with no oil (*and you know who you are*) get some oil while the oil is being pressed out! *Receive ye the power of the Holy Ghost to tread upon the lion and the adder, to endure tribulation, to work miracles in front of those who doubt the faith so that they might believe, that ye may endure to the end by Faith, Amen.*

Have ye heard of the power miracles that the Lord God performed in front of the Hebrews through the hands of Moses? With the faith that my brother, Moses, had and what he allowed God do was amazing, *God be praised.* For the same Spirit of the Man who was in Moses was the same that came and dwelt among flesh! I pray that ye go with me lastly to a set of scriptures to see more of the power of faith and what it can do when you have it. Go to *Exodus 34:1-8, And the LORD said unto Moses,*

¹ Hew thee two tables of stone like unto the first: and I will write upon these tables the words that were in the first tables, which thou brakest.

² And be ready in the morning, and come up in the morning unto mount Sinai, and present thyself there to me in the top of the mount.

³ And no man shall come up with thee, neither let any man be seen throughout all the mount; neither let the flocks nor herds feed before that mount.

⁴ And he hewed two tables of stone like unto the first; and Moses rose up early in the morning, and went up unto mount Sinai, as the LORD had commanded him, and took in his hand the two tables of stone.

⁵ And the LORD descended in the cloud, and stood with him there, and proclaimed the name of the LORD.

⁶ And the LORD passed by before him, and proclaimed, The LORD, The LORD God, merciful and gracious, longsuffering, and abundant in goodness and truth,

⁷ Keeping mercy for thousands, forgiving iniquity and transgression and sin, and that will by no means clear the guilty; visiting the iniquity of the fathers upon the children, and upon the children's children, unto the third and to the fourth generation.

⁸ And Moses made haste, and bowed his head toward the earth, and worshipped.

The LORD came unto Moses and spoke saying that He would appear to Him, and by the faith of Moses the Lord God appeared before him. We see some of the character of the Lord knowing Who Himself is as the wonderful LORD God of heaven, full of mercy and truth, the forgiver of all sins, *Amen*. We can see that by Moses having the faith that He had believing and trusting that the King would come like He said He came. If Moses didn't have the faith and didn't want the Lord to appear He most likely wouldn't have for the lack of faith that he would've had. Moses went in expecting something from the Lord and because he did he came out with "new" commandments from the Lord for His people.

That is what faith is expecting, believing, hoping, and trusting the Lord that He can and *has already done what you asked for, even though it hasn't happened yet.* You see it in the Spirit yet claim it with your mouth, speaking what the Lord has promised in the atmosphere in faith *like it has already been completed of what ye asked the Lord of hosts to do,* Amen. Many don't believe that we can speak things into existence, why would deny yourself the power that the Father gave you? Have ye not read the scripture my friends? That that tongue has power the speak life or death*(Proverbs 18:21).* Look at out Lord He is the Life and look at how He spoke life into existence, and look at the devil he gets in one of the gates*(mind, ear, eye, mouth gates)* and can cause you to speak death(literal or spiritual death, defeat, negativity, curses, etc.)out of your mouth. We must remember friends that this is a spiritual walk more that so it is physical, what happens in the spiritual shows up in our physical lives. Why do you think that what you speak is so important? Once we have become *living spirits* no longer *dead* spiritually having full consciousness of the God of heaven and earth, what we speak we are *even the more so* held accountable. *Because* we are spiritual aware we need to be careful what we speak because we have the godliness bestowed back in us by *the Holy Ghost*, since we are living spirits, like I said *spiritual aware* and we have faith which is spiritual what we speak makes its way quicker to the physical. Understand this that there are two sides to the spiritual either you are spiritually alive in the Light of the Lord, or spiritually dead in the darkness with Satan there is no in between. Those of you who are supposed to be the mothers of the church women of God, the fathers of the church all men and women who are supposedly of God yet you go out *from* praise and worship gossiping about your fellowservant of God. And you wonder why you have you ailments? Also those whom you speak against they can't seem to get out of their rut because you speak against them, but God is about to shift things and He is about to vindicate those of your brethren whom you demean behind their back. Not only that, but then put on the *face of love* yet underneath you are miserable yourself.

Faith in God is the only way to getting what He promised you, for worry will not get you anywhere! For you cannot pray then worry for your prayer will literally bounce around, for when you release the prayer let it be of a beautiful incense unto the Lord. Allow Him to breathe in your words and let Him take care of your needs my friends! For we wonder why no one is being pulled out of wheelchairs, why no one is being healed from sickness, why people are losing their lives, because the Church has put down the very tool that we need to have the Lord work on our behalves, that is *faith*. Without faith(which the world doesn't have) all things are impossible, but with God and having the faith in Him that He can do the things that you need Him to do *all things and I mean **all things** are possible, Hallelujah Amen!* For my faith in the King of Life is what kept me here on this earth for without Him I'd be dead and gone! I got stricken by the evil one a horrible sickness, pneumonia which almost cost me my life, but the Lord said, "*Not so! For I have plans for your life!*"

Before I got sick, I had *just* received His Spirit at a conference and I had faith and told the Lord that there is *no way* that this could be it and that it was not over. Not once by His Grace did I think about death, nor was I afraid of it! For the Lord and His Grace I received *through faith* to be able to breathe and write unto you this day! Hallelujah, Amen for He is the Rock in the weary land, when I thought all was lost, my life was over, He stepped in and turned that sickness into health! I stand before you to say that with faith *only in Jesus Christ the One and True God* is the reason I am here, and this *is* the reason *why He kept me, Amen thank You Jesus!!!* Selah.

One thing I want to say to the Church of today is that there is no need to *covet* and want the things that your brother or sister has! There is no *need* to be jealous of them, for you have greatness inside(*placed there by God*) and there are things that the King wants to do for you. You don't need to measure yourself to anyone else, for you are one of a kind in the Lord *focus*, my friends, *focus on the Lord Jesus Christ and not man.*

Have ye read about the faith on the centurion? How he had so much faith in the Lord that if He said to do this that he would send his servant to do this or that for Him to save his servants life? Read the passage along with me friends, for this faith that centurion had was great! Will you have faith in the Lord like this or even greater? Do you still believe that He can still do things today?? Flip to Matthew 8:5-13,

5 And when Jesus was entered into Capernaum, there came unto him a centurion, beseeching him,

6 And saying, Lord, my servant lieth at home sick of the palsy, grievously tormented.

7 And Jesus saith unto him, I will come and heal him.

8 The centurion answered and said, Lord, I am not worthy that thou shouldest come under my roof: but speak the word only, and my servant shall be healed.

9 For I am a man under authority, having soldiers under me: and I say to this man, Go, and he goeth; and to another, Come, and he cometh; and to my servant, Do this, and he doeth it.

10 When Jesus heard it, he marvelled, and said to them that followed, Verily I say unto you, I have not found so great faith, no, not in Israel.

11 And I say unto you, That many shall come from the east and west, and shall sit down with Abraham, and Isaac, and Jacob, in the kingdom of heaven.

12 But the children of the kingdom shall be cast out into outer darkness: there shall be weeping and gnashing of teeth.

13 And Jesus said unto the centurion, Go thy way; and as thou hast believed, so be it done unto thee. *And his servant was healed in the selfsame hour.*

Our Lord *marvelled* at the centurion's faith, saying in terms that you can understand if you do not, "I am not worthy enough to have you in my home, Lord if you say the words it'll happen my servant shall be healed." Look at this my friends, sometimes from where you are whether it be in the marketplace, in a spiritual storm, in a whole bunch of mess with faith all you gotta say is, "Lord, just say the words and it's already done." or "Lord, just say the words and I am healed," "Say the words Lord and my Mom is healed, my dad, grandma, all my loved ones." Suffer not that He come to where you are go to where He is in His Presence in expectation and with fire knowing that the King of kings will surely do it *before* you ask. For this faith will move mountains from their foundations, heal the sick, cast out demons, fire fall from heaven, cause the Lord to *marvel* at your faith. I don't know about you, *my friends*, but all I want to do is please the Father to be a beautiful sight to His eyes, and what I do for Him be of a sweet savouring smell unto His nostrils. Do you want to please Him? Do want to see the mountains move from their foundations? Do you want to see the sick healed? Do you want to see the lame walk, run, and shout? Have faith in God! And not in man for faith in God with all your heart is the only way to see Him work, and not to prohibit His work and what He wants to do for you and others. I pray that right now in the Mighty Name of the Lord Jesus Christ that whatever is hindering your faith I bind it right now by the power of the Holy Ghost and send it to the pit of hell where it belongs! Now faith in the substance of things hoped for and the evidence of things not seen(*to the natural eye!*). In this season I challenge you to have faith like you've never had before and watch Him work wonderous things in your life! Amen and Amen for the Lord God of Heaven and Earth is good and is worthy to be praised for no other God, no other Son, nor other Spirit deserves the praise, glory, or honor for we serve One Lord, have One Faith, in One Body, One Spirit, believing in One God and Father who is over all, through all, and in all, Amen. Selah!

Here's another scripture about faith and what it can do, I just want you to see that there are no boundaries when it comes to God and the faith that you have depends on your willingness to see this, that *literally all things are possible with the Lord God of heaven, Hallelujah Amen!* Let's take a look at Luke 18:35-43,

35 And it came to pass, that as he was come nigh unto Jericho, a certain blind man sat by the wayside begging:

36 And hearing the multitude pass by, he asked what it meant.

37 And they told him, that Jesus of Nazareth passeth by.

38 And he cried, saying, Jesus, thou son of David, have mercy on me.

39 And they which went before rebuked him, that he should hold his peace: but he cried so much the more, Thou son of David, have mercy on me.

40 And Jesus stood, and commanded him to be brought unto him: and when he was come near, he asked him,

⁴¹ *Saying,* *What wilt thou that I shall do unto thee?* *And he said,* *Lord, that I may receive my sight.*

⁴² *And Jesus said unto him,* *Receive thy sight: thy faith hath saved thee.*

⁴³ *And immediately he received his sight, and followed him, glorifying God: and all the people, when they saw it, gave praise unto God.*

Faith cometh by hearing *the word of God*, and the blind men heard *the LORD, the Word of God* was passing by and they had the faith to call out to God to receive their healing! This is such a beautiful passage that it brings me to tears, because these men not being able to see, only hearing of the healer they took a chance on the King of kings, and He had compassion on them and healed them instantly for their faith was indeed *instant* when they heard of Him. For as I stated before that our God is a God of immediacy, and does things immediately at the time that is asked or when He sees fit, but when He gives He gives out of pleasure with all fullness, *even more than what you asked for.* He is our God and our King and we are His people He *wants and desires* that we are in good health, have what we need when it comes to necessities: food, clothes, water, money, etc. Don't think that the God of Heaven and Earth cannot supply these things unto you my friends for He *is the God of the Heavens and the Earth*, so why wouldn't He be able to supply *earthly* things to you? Him being just that how could He not be Christ? When Christ confessed that He was *the Son of God*? The God of Heaven *in the flesh, and still comes in the flesh(these are the true descendants of Abraham those who are born of the Spirit by faith in Christ Jesus, God alone. Amen!)* The title *Son of God* shows God's humanity, and that He was indeed Christ! Look at the accusation of the Pharisees, *"The Jews answered him, saying, For a good work we stone thee not; but for blasphemy; and because that thou, being a man, makest thyself God."(John 10:33).* Now, look at what they said *'thou, being a man, makest thyself God,'* not the Son of God(even though He is, this symbolizes His coming in the flesh so I adjure you don't get it twisted allow me to further explain the matter of our Lord and Saviour Christ and His Sonship with the Father) they are saying that He is claiming to be the Almighty God *who was and is to come*. The One at the beginning, Who called everything to be, this is why the demonic forces *bowed to Christ* confessing *Who He was*. Look with the eyes of the Spirit my friends, the LORD God Almighty shushed them that they wouldn't make Him known until it was time, also so that He could further explain *Who He was* so that they may receive full revelation from the Father God of Heaven and Earth(*this is why He has the title because Him dwelling in the heavens, coming and being revealed also in the earth as Christ Jesus the True King of Israel, over all Jews and Gentiles, Amen and Amen!*).

This sort of revelation comes by faith in the Spirit of God to show you that you may understand the mysteries of Christ! Me being a man do not have the keys to unlock this knowledge on my own, but I have *access to the Father by One Spirit* and that is *Christ Who is the Father. So I have access to the knowledge of Christ by Christ, Who is the Spirit that took upon flesh, the Holy One of Israel, the Holy Ghost who shed His blood for us*(Acts 20:28, please read so that you may have understanding and have it full by the fullness of Christ, Amen). Praise God for His Oneness and giving us access through His Son by Faith in Him. Faith unlocks doors, and brings you to *greater heights in Christ* and brings the provision that you have created for yourself by the will of God making it a reality in your life. God's goodness towards us and us being able to receive starts with us first, with the faith of a mustard seed we can conquer things, His Power and Goodness both will be displayed all we have to do is believe in Christ Jesus and He will do what we ask of Him. Come boldly to the throne of Grace by faith and remind the Lord of Whose child you are, and who is your Father. That He may do as He promised us, He has to because as His *beloved* He *has* to do what He promised because *we are His*. He wouldn't be the God that He said He is, *Jehovah Jireh, or God our Provider*. Let your heart not be hardened against God when things seem to be not going the way *you* would like it to, whether you be sick, in debt, homeless even, because we must remember we give up *our lives* to live a life full of Christ. He is the Father, and He is Who started a good work in you, and He is able to complete that work in you! Will you let Him brothers and sisters? Or will you give up? Will you allow Satan to cause you to leave Christ because things seem to not turning around?

We must push forward even when things seem to be going wrong *God the Lord Jesus Christ is GOD the LORD!* Don't doubt the King! We have more faith in our parents than we do God. Why do you think that He is called the Father, because we are His children and He takes care of us. Just as you know that no matter what when Dad or Mom gets home you are going to eat, you have "blind faith" almost in that fact that you know that they are going to do what they say. In that same fashion we should *even the more* trust God, because our parents can fail, and they will more as they go throughout their lives, but God is a Father that cannot fail who would you rather have more faith in? If you are sick and you know that God is the Healer, you hurriedly make your way to the hospital to see a doctor when you haven't spoken to the One Who created nor prayed concerning your situation. And you wonder why your not healed? Why God isn't moving? Because where there is no faith, there is no access for Him to work in your life. Simple as that my friends. Give the Lord Jesus Christ access in your life by having faith in Him to do what it is that He promised, that you asked and He approved of. Why? As I stated before our God is *capable* to do these things because He is the LORD(Supreme Ruler) GOD(Creator) of the Heavens and the Earth. Have faith in Him for whatever it is that you may be struggling with whether it be financial, pornography, mental health, homosexuality, lesbianism, sickness, diseases, anger, bitterness etc. and watch Him work in your life. Remember my friends YOU MUST HAVE FAITH IN HIM FOR HIM TO WORK not if, ands, or buts about it. No faith, no promise. No faith, no access! God Bless you all may you be blessed in your coming in, go out and in the field. Our victory is within our reach, look not so much to the things of this world, but to the things of Christ, the Spirit of God, Amen.

4. *Access through the blood of the Lamb*

Since we now understand as children of God, Who our God is, and what He came to do and by faith in Him we can accomplish many things by His Power. I pray that you are starting to see Whose you are and how special you are to Him, your Father in heaven. Are you *still* struggling? Are there some sinful desires still within you? Is your heart still broken? Those of you that have heard the Father's voice through my words, you are here you made it to chapter four or else you'd still be confused.(With saying that you may just need clarity of all the last three chapters, ask the Holy Spirit to help you to understand who the Father is with the Son, and explain all that He gave, I guarantee that He will do it!)

God be praised for blessing His servants with such knowledge of His Son, the mysteries of the kingdom of God, Amen.

Know this that whatever you struggle with, whether it be lack of understanding His Word, completion in understanding the mysteries of Christ, confusion, know this that the Lamb of God shed His blood along with the Holy Ghost(*Acts 20:28*) on the cross at Calvary for you to break the vale to break the wall of sin between God and man. The Ghost of the Lamb fills His people with His Spirit and reveals what He will concerning Himself and the Father, give no room to the enemy understand that you now have access through One Spirit to the Father and that is the Holy Ghost of the Lamb, Christ Jesus. Listen not to the accusations and lies of Satan, the traditions of your pastors that you cannot hear the voice of God directly. Once you have accepted Christ in your heart and Him as Lord and Savior you now have access to that very thing, you have overcome by the blood of the Lamb, and by your testimony of Him ye shall also overcome what you are used to doing, the sins and stronghold that hold you so dearly.

Christ has called us into a place of reconciliation unto Himself, to God that we may be a part of His body and hear Him, have *access to Him.* All sin surrenders itself to the Jesus Christ and the power of His blood. Death is no longer the result of our lives if we are living accordingly to the life that Christ our Father has built for His children. God no longer sees the spots that stained you from sin, but sees you as whole, healed, delivered, and reconciled back unto Himself(once you've accepted Him in your soul). Why was it the will of the Father for us to believe on the Son of God? Why did Jesus go through the motions of teaching us about us being His sheep? Because Christ is the Father and the Father is Christ, God showed us His Love that was always in Christ Jesus who was, and is to come in the end of the beginning(our new beginning with Him). We also saw Christ the Father as a brother to those who believed on Him, showing us to the kind of relationship that He desired to have with His children, a friendship even. Even though He is King He wants to give us access to Him without so much as a prophet, or pastor always having to speak to God for you to get an answer but He requires all of us to get a personal relationship with Him as King,

Brother, Father and Friend. But we must be careful that we don't forget that like I mentioned He is King and the Father and we must respect Him as such. He is never to be on the same level as your brothers here on earth He was lifted up on High as God the Father and that is Who He will always be revealed in Christ, may He reign forever and ever, Amen.

I pray that you no longer allow Satan to accuse you, or rather let it bother you, once you have come to the Father's feet for forgiveness through the Son you are forgiven and have been made free by His Hands only. *Therefore if the Son makes you free, you shall be free indeed.(John 8:36).* No one can pluck you out of the Father's Hand, nor the Hand of the Son because He is your keeper, your Protector, your Provider, so therefore with saying this no man on earth or principality in the heavens or below can separate your from the love of God found in Christ. His Love is what keeps us in that place of access to Him, we cannot sin and expect to be close to Him as we would when we are following His statutes(just as our father David did in his day).

Let the peace of God rule your hearts friends! Listen not to the negatives about what you have done and how you are non-deservant of the things which He has done and is doing for you, you are made deservant by receiving His Son, therefore His Grace and Mercy. Isaiah 53:5 says this,

⁵ But he was wounded for our transgressions, he was bruised for our iniquities: the chastisement of our peace was upon him; and with his stripes we are healed.

Allow the peace that Jesus gave to His disciples rule your hearts, because God has called us to a place of peace! Our past lives should matter not to us because it is not *us that live, no, but Christ liveth in us*(Galatians 5:20-21). And no we don't or should not frustrate the grace of God, because if we do what it is that required without heart it is null in vain and *Christ is dead in vain.* Know this, *you are free in Jesus the Father's Holy Name, Amen!(The reference of words comes from the KJV study Bible.)*Let the work of Christ and what *He did* rule your heart and mind for these are *the heavenly things* that we should be looking forward to and thinking upon, *not the things of this world but the things that are praiseworthy, Amen Lord!* Keep what Christ did it the forefront of your mind everyday recall what He, the Father, His sacrifice up upon that cross was for you and I, the love that was shed for us! He thought that we were *worth* dying for, *worth saving, worth raising up out of the grave for.* Do ye not understand yet that you have been made *free* by His sacrifice? Why do ye still fear?! Be ye made perfect in the love of the Father found in Christ that you may be free mentally, physically, and spiritually in the name of the Father, and of the Son, and of the Holy Ghost, in the name of the One came in the name of the Lord, Christ Jesus, Amen. Don't let Satan keep you bound with accusations friends for he is a liar and the father of them and doesn't know the truth from a lie, he cannot know it, so rather listen to the Advocate, the Spirit of Christ the Father that died for you saying, " *My child, I have set you free from bondage, never return for I have made you whole inside and out. You shall never be the same for your Father has made you clean, just as a Shepherd cleans and washes His sheep until they are clean.*" saith the Lord God of Heaven, the Father in Heaven and in the Earth, Selah and Amen. Hallelujah! Be to the One Who sits on the throne of Glory!

By the blood of the Lamb we are set free, for His blood was the symbol of the ultimate sacrifice made for us unto God for our salvation. We are His children and He wants us to understand everything that He has done for us and why. You may think in your mind, *"Who is this guy? That he would have such knowledge of these things?"* I say unto you my friends please be not offended of me for I am only the messenger of God, His Servant bound unto Him, a servant and fellow-heir in Christ with you, and just like you I am but a man searching to understand my God in and out. To take hold of the knowledge that He gives unto you, He has given me such knowledge to spread to those who will receive it in their hearts and minds, and may have the fullness of the knowledge of the Son of God, God the Father, and the Holy Ghost of God. That you be made whole in the One True God that is Christ Jesus. Praise God!

Continuing on my friends you must recognize and understand by the Spirit of God that our God is not a God that can be recognized only revealed. So with the revelation that I have received I will now make it plain unto you what the Father in heaven has shown His son and servant. Starting at the beginning in Genesis with Abel and Cain, really focusing on Cain with the sacrificial offerings that God called and set forth, atoning for their sins with blood. If there is no blood shed no sacrifice, so you can see our God; the first "*hints*" of Christ our Lord. God knew in the beginning that there would need to be a sacrifice made for man. So being the intuitive and wise God that He was and *is*, He showed us that the daily sacrifices that we made back in the day for ourselves would never be enough. Let me put this more plainly, absolutely NOTHING that we do could EVER wash our sin away completely. The animals that God created for the man has no conscious soul, as in a knowledge of word or religious sense. So in that case we pull together and we know now that they go off of instinct not personal will. God showed us this so that He came as His soul and heart, *Christ Jesus*, that He was the *only way* to Himself to be cleansed through His conscious sacrifice!

Do you see the difference? What made God's sacrifice so special and powerful was because He was God first of all, then the sacrifice He made was a conscious decision. And unlike an animal He knew what He was doing and where He was going, and that was to the slaughterhouse, and He did it *willingly*. God told me as I mentioned before that the blood of Jesus was the symbol of that the sacrifice was made and that His blood instead of it cleaning man's sin for a day or however long the Lord permitted for an animal sacrifice, it covered all sin for eternity! Do you see how powerful it is?! So when you plead the blood of Jesus, you are asking God for His power that He showed through His Son at Calvary my friends! It's not just part of an old hymn but it should be a highly significant part in the Christian man or woman's lives. So when Satan brings sickness against you and your family you say, 'The blood of Jesus!' Or rather, 'The blood of Jesus is against it!' Because when the demons hear that they have to flee because the power that you are pleading is an ancient power and anointing, and they have to honor it by leaving you alone. And they have no more power over you, because the price has already been paid for you so that darkness no longer can take from you my friends. The reason why I say ancient is because God did this a long while ago, so you are accessing the ancient power that He already bestowed for you to grab a hold of. Thank You Jesus! Thank Him for the blood that He shed for us brothers and sisters! Those of you who were atheists, but are now changing your minds thank the Lord Jesus Christ for His sacrifice! But those of you who are reading this and are still dwelling in darkness, and are still bitter against your God may He reveal Himself to you by His power in a different way through dreams or however He wills. Now you may be offended when I said you are still in darkness, but my God is Light so the opposite side is darkness and those of you who have chosen Him dwell in the Light my friends.

Anyhow, those of you have made it here and are receiving more revelation from the Lord God, know this going furthermore, especially those of you who have just started learning that through the sacrifice of God our Savior, Jesus Christ, we have access now to Him because He was the ultimate sacrifice for us! Went as a sheep with His mouth shut not uttering a harsh word, not even a word at all and willingly went and died for our sins. When He began to be slandered, bruised and beaten our healing began, so did our iniquities begin to vanish, and to tie a bow on it when He died the sacrifice that He was making was complete. Understand deeper my friends! Our healing from the power of darkness that we gave it, our sicknesses, our iniquities and transgressions were completely erased! GONE! Immediately! And to show us that He willingly died for our sins He *gave up the ghost (Check out John 19:30)*. Now how can a man willingly give up his spirit? Only the One Who has the power of life in His hands can do so brothers and sisters and other readers, *He gave it up. Willingly.* Jesus being the Master Prophet and the Mighty God of Life He prophesied that He would do this! Let's go to scripture!

John 10:18, *[18] No man taketh it from me, but I lay it down of myself. I have power to lay it down, and I have power to take it again. This commandment have I received of my Father.*

Going forward we must understand that no one, and I mean no one else in the Bible had this power given to them(or has been given this commandment to do so friends). We must always refer to scripture as reference because in the Lord's Word there is truth running throughout. His Word states, *The Lord giveth and He taketh away blessed be the name of the Lord(Read the scripture in its entirety Job 1:21).* In this case, brothers and sisters to make it clear guys only God can give or take life.

Why? Because He is the Creator, the giver of life itself, Jesus Christ, was and is the Only God that can do this my friends. He is the Father, the Son, and the Holy Ghost friends and Jesus Christ is His Name.

Look here in John 12:27-28, *27 Now is my soul troubled; and what shall I say? Father, save me from this hour: but for this cause came I unto this hour.*

28 Father, glorify thy name. **Then came there a voice from heaven, saying, I have both glorified it, and will glorify it again.**

Pay attention you scholars, pastors of different doctrines from the true faith of Jesus Christ, the Father here responds to His Name that was given to His Son, He is both unified and glorified in the heavens and the earth claim ownership of His Name and Deity. Just in case you are still in doubt I shall bring you to another scripture by the Holy Ghost to cut away that doubt and to diminish your pride in your false religion and belief. In your Bibles(because I know that some of you will go to the scriptures to ensure that I am quoting the correct passage. And some not for confirmation, nor for understanding but in anger to ensure that the words line up to try to misquote me, but I speak the Word of God with truth, and the Word of Life does not lie nor can it be contridicted my friends.) remain in the book of John my friends jump a few chapters over to John 17:3-6, *3 And this is life eternal, that they might know thee the only true God, and Jesus Christ, whom thou hast sent.*

4 I have glorified thee on the earth: I have finished the work which thou gavest me to do.

5 And now, O Father, glorify thou me with thine own self with the glory which I had with thee before the world was.

6 I have manifested thy name unto the men which thou gavest me out of the world: thine they were, and thou gavest them me; and they have kept thy word.

We see here that this is God the Father incarnated as the Son of God, so jumping back to my original point this was no ordinary man, but the Ultimate Son of God, God Himself in the flesh! So Him being a man that knew no sin, this just make sense (if you have captured the understanding and revelation in your hearts) that this *is* indeed God. So His blood was unbelievably pure, His soul was not tainted at all by the darkness of sin, not one drop stained His Spirit, for He was the God Incarnate and sacrificed Himself for His people. Let me ask you a question as in kingdom wise. If a King is not willing to sacrifice Himself for His people is He really a True King? There is no honor in a king that is not willing to do so. But our King Who is King of the heavenlies and of the earth willingly came down *stripping Himself of His visible glory* and died for your sins! O LORD how great Thou art! For your blood can make the rivers of Jordan clear as glass, your sweat on your brow and whips on your back can cure the maidenwoman from her sickness and barrenness! Your the Great King of the world, and of the Jews, the man of God Who was the Son of God, and now ascended back unto the Father! Amen!

God sent forth His heart and soul to be put on the line, to be bruised for you, something that He held close to His heart which was His own Heart and Soul, Himself Jesus Christ! Remember, *But He was wounded for our transgressions, He bruised for our iniquities: for the chastisement of our peace was upon Him; and with His stripes we are healed.* Amen. Let the peace of God rule in your hearts, as ye are called unto One body, be thankful(*Colossians 3:15*)
. Having the peace and joy knowing that through the sacrifice of our Savior and King we are free! And healed by every stripe that He took! Praise the Lord God! Hallelujah! Through His Holy Blood we are cleansed from all sin, and broken free from the power of it. Thank you Jesus for Your Mighty Sacrifice we as Your Church will be forever grateful, even when we ascend in greatness beholding Your Glory given from Your Father whom has glorified Thy Name we will shout praises recalling what You've done O Lord for the rest of eternity. For we shall say, 'Howdy, howdy, praise ye the God of the heavens and the earth! Amen.' For those of you who are now accepting Jesus Christ, whether it be for the first time or with full knowledge of Who He is, may His blood cleanse you in and out, breaking you free from the bondage of sin, and the chains of your iniquities. Amen, be glorified O Mighty God of Zion! Once you are cleansed by His Blood you are made pure, making you white as snow in His eyes. The Savior died for our sin yes, but, however, whatever sins that commit we mustn't forget to take account for them.

We must acknowledge them to our King, you've already been cleansed by the Lord's Blood, and because of that you can go to His throne boldly confessing your faults to Him. You are acknowledging them, and when you go to Him you are acknowledging that His sacrifice is enough to cover what you've done. Praise God for being our Propitiation that we may have our sins remitted(and washed away) unto to the Father so that we can maintain our freedom in Christ Jesus, Amen. Glory to the Most High God and to His Right Hand. Selah.

5. Grace, Mercy, and Favor

Praise the Lord God Jehovah! For He is mighty in the land, mighty in all the earth, powerful and strong in the heavens. For He hath given you the grace to continue in this book, and by His Favor towards you have received the full knowledge of who the Son of God *was and is*, and by His Mercy you have been made whole in the understanding of the power of tongues, have become aware of *the false doctrines*, and finally you have understood that by the sacrifice of Jesus the Christ you are cleansed by His blood and receiving Him into your heart, soul and mind. Amen.

A lot of people may wonder what is the difference between Grace and Mercy allow me by the Holy Ghost of God to break it down to you. Through obedience to God the Father His Grace along with Favor is shown in a way for you to be able to do certain things He allows. This is a form of His kindness being shown towards His people, those of us who take heed to His Word. Now Mercy even though it does go hand in hand with Grace there is a slight difference between the two. Do you recall in the book of Jonah when the King allowed His prophet by His Grace to go and speak a word of prophecy unto the people of Nineveh? God sent the prophet to speak unto them and give them warning of the coming invasion. At first Jonah *"fled from the presence of the Lord"* because he didn't want to go what the Lord had commanded of him because He was afraid. He realized after being swallowed by the large fish that the Lord God was the God of the earth and sea that he could not escape the presence of the Lord. And that he was the one called to do this for the Lord, no one else. So the Lord came a second time and told him to go to Nineveh and warn the people! God(*the Lord at first had Mercy with Jonah for running from the Lord through his repentance, the Lord God could have easily allowed the prophet to remain in the fish's stomach and die but also because of the Favor He has with God, He remembered Him and had the fish to vomit him up onto the sand*) gave him the Grace to be able to continue and speak to the people concerning the invasion, and when the people heard what was going to happen if they did not repent they turned to the God of heaven and of Zion for their salvation! Now this is Mercy, when God should allow this to happen because of the lack of the repentance of sin He refrains from allowing things such as sickness, or, in this case an invasion from happening. And with saying that Grace or His Kindness was given to allow their hearts to return through the Word of God, then also too they found Favor in the sight of God.

So by the Grace of God you preachers, teachers, prophets, evangelists and you apostles you have been given this great gift to preach the Word of God! As the Bible says not all are preachers and all the other things that I have listed but *we are all ministers of the Gospel*. But especially talking to them who are in those particular offices you need to be in your office not just when it's your turn to be in the pulpit. And what I mean by that is just in case you don't understand for those of you are still trying to understand who you are in God, you need to do the necessary things to make sure you maintain the office to which you were called to my friends, very simple. Grace should be where you and I as people who have accepted Christ this is where we should stand. Mercy is shown *every morning* to those who are in sin twenty-four seven, and like the people of Nineveh when they turned to God. Favor like Grace is found in obedience unto God my friends. Now if you perceive through the Spirit of God what I am saying, praise God, for the Father is not the author of confusion but of Peace. We are all given *new mercies* every morning as a refresher for the day before. Even those of you who are atheists you also too receive *new mercies every morning from the Lord*. He loves you regardless of your hate for Him.

So with those of you who are in sin you live and breath by the everlasting mercies of God, but us Christians live by the Grace of God with Favor from on High. Amen. People of God with the Grace that we are given do not waste it nor crucify Christ again and again by going back to the taskmaster, that is sin(*which is the devil*). I ask that you live life accordingly to how God in Christ lived. Will there be mistakes? Yes, my friends surely there shall be because we must first remember that we were born into sin, it was once comfortable and the Light coming in disturbs your "*peace*" while you were yet sleeping in the darkness. Now, your eyes are open to the *Great Light that is Christ Jesus*(see in John 1:4-9). Why do some of us wish to go back to sleep in the darkness, not be aware of the great things ahead? *Because* we are no longer awake but we have allowed ourselves to go back into a daze while trying to live in the Light, in Christ Jesus our God. God says unto you, *"Come on my children, remain awake for great things are ahead."* Some of us rather go back to sleep in the darkness because it feels better to you. Don't think so? Answer me this question. When you are asleep in the physical and someone comes and opens the blinds bringing in the sunlight how do you react?

This is something that everyone(including myself) does! I either roll over, or ask them to close the blinds, even *turn off the light.* This is what some of us are telling God, *"Turn off the Light! It's too bright!"* Or even, *" I am trying to sleep!"* Beware my siblings in Christ, for you are falling from Grace right into the hands of Mercy, losing the Favor as the little sheep of the Father that you once had with Him. You have pushed Daddy away so that you can go back to sleep, your fight in the Spirit is weak. The enemy tosses you around easily and because of this you'd rather return back to your slumber, which is darkness and sin *because* it is more comfortable for you that way. I praise God for those you who are still(*as the saints of God*) are living by faith and obedience in the favor and everlasting Grace of our King, King Jesus the Christ. Amen. The Blood of Jesus covers you from head to toe, do not allow yourselves to fall back into sin, no longer *sin willingly but crucify your flesh at the cross with Christ(Galatians 5:20).* I pray right now over you saints, myself included lastly, that you will allow God to protect you from the deceptive ways and powers of darkness that are so ever present in today's world that you hold up the blood-stained banner of Christ; that you hold it with joy and boldness in your Lord. *God has not given us a spirit of fear, but of power, and of love, and of a sound mind(2 Timothy 1:7).* Fear not the jailhouses, nor their prisons, nor their bashing, nor their hatred for all that has been overcome by the One and True Savior, Jesus Christ. *Everything* that is attacking the True Christian faith has been subjected *under His feet.* LGBT, homosexuality, perversion, evil lusts, and abominations, guns, even our government and their control has been subjected *under* our God's feet. So why are we afraid to speak the truth and *not* sugar coat it? Why are we trying to impress the world and not the God that we serve? It's because we have allowed sin to enter into the Church! We are falling from Grace, Favor, and Obedience right into the hands of Mercy which are meant for the evildoers not the saints my friends! We are to preach and do what we do for the kingdom of God regardless to other communities commands. At the end of the day we *do not* answer to them but to the God of heaven! I fear and respect my God more than I do anyone, can you say the same? Are you still ashamed? Are you worried if those few members that joined who serve the LGBT community will leave? This is what it comes down to, you will either serve God or Satan there is no God-satan, nor is there *any grey area* but it is either Light or darkness! Which one do you choose? Make a choice now for what is to come you will have needed to be serving our God or theirs by that time. May God be praised for His chastisement and love towards us to come to us with such authority and power.

I am not afraid to do such things, for Satan has absolutely no power nor does he have any strongholds in the True Church. Nor can he demand anything of me and I have to bow to his will. That is unthinkable! God's Will is the *only* Will that I will fulfill in my life, mine has been crucified with Christ and I am no longer a slave to sin, but a slave to Christ where there is freedom in His Spirit. I'd rather be bound by Light rather than my own darkness and sin. Even though it may seem good, I pray that by the grace of God He keeps me from it. Do I want to sin? Of course not! But will it happen? Yes it will, but instead of me staying in that sin I must return to Grace and Favor in Obedience that I may not fall into the Mighty Hands of Mercy. Amen.

Receive ye the grace of God today, receive Christ in your heart that you may live by the way of obedience that you may reap the benefits of Light rather than recompense the wages of darkness. I pray thee lay down your burdens of what you have done over the past few years for I know that they have been rough on you, but you needn't not do this alone my friend trust in God and He will deliver you through His Son, Christ Jesus, fulfill all your needs and work out the desires of your heart. For I am sure that God being the God that He is, He will gladly and surely as your Father take care of His own. I love each and everyone of you whether you be blasphemers and atheists according to the doctrine of Christ Jesus, or being a Spirit-filled baptized with fire saint of God, *I love you with the Love of God which He hath placed in me.* I pray that ye love me the same, for we are One Body called unto One Spirit to the Father, let us lay down our pride and jealousy against one another and be the children of God *together*, not in *separate communities(as in baptists, methodists, trinitarians, catholics, pentecostals)*. Amen. Praise God!

In order to receive the Favor of God through obedience you must be steadfast, remaining in prayer and watching, always in the Word of

God that ye may grow and bloom in the Spirit of the Living God the Holy One. *Favor isn't fair!* You've probably heard this saying but is is true and *it does* have some significance to it, because not everyone including the "*saints of God*" are, so to some of those who are church don't receive Favor from God because they still are dwelling in sin. Just like the Sadducees and Pharisees they were supposed to men and women of God yet they hated the Holy One which was sent before them, why? Because they were living deep in sin as heretics, therefore this easily gave way for jealousy to enter their hearts and have their minds full of vain and cruel imaginations towards God when He came on the earth. They received Him not as God, but tried to compare him to the beasts of this world, the men who love darkness and love inventing evil schemes to trap the innocent. They tried making an incorruptible God a corruptible man(*Romans 1:19-25*)! *Jesus Christ, being the truth of God they tried to turn it into an evil lie being filled with indignation against the One and Only God of Zion(John 14:6)!*

Let us come under subjection under one God, one Lord/LORD, under one Faith, and baptizing with one Baptism, into one Body all subjected under the feet and the salvation of Jesus Christ. Who was the Image of the Invisible God brought forth as God as a man in flesh, yet totally walked in the Spirit of God(Colossians 1:15-23). No longer shall we be called trinitarians, be those who are of polytheism belief that there are two gods, nor shall we be those who know the truth but don't preach or teach it but we should be named Christ Jesus. For in Him dwelleth the body, and He is the head and without Him we could not function as a Body! So let us be one just as He and His Father are one, let us be one in each other even as they are indeed One Person and Body(*John 17:10-12,21-26, even their name is the same, making them equally One Person, Body, Spirit, God and Lord because there is none like the Lord! We see the power of the Almighty His Presence simultaneously here on earth and in the heavens at the same time! Our God is good isn't He? Let the Spirit wrap your mind around it, because your effort to do will end in error and lack of understanding! Praise God, Amen!*). I hope that your understanding thus far has brought you to the fullness of the Lord. Because it is your Father's desire that you know Who He is, not ever question Who He is but know altogether, never in part Who He is. And that is Christ Jesus is the Lord of hosts and glory, Who divided the Red Sea for Moses, and the One Who reigned fire on Elijah's enemies, and He Who brought our ancestors back from slavery. This is Jesus Christ! He was once along with creation hidden, but when He came upon the earth as His heart and soul it was all made clear Who our God was. That He is a Man, the LORD from the Old Testament, the Truth, the Way to restoration and righteousness, and the way to Life(*through obedience and subjecting yourselves to Him, Amen!*).

Through obedience will Favor come, only through obedience and surrenderance will healing and Grace come upon you my friends. God only trust very that He has chosen with such knowledge of Him, those who can hear of it take it and grasp it and use it for the betterment of the church and the restoration of the world. Many will come prophesying, teaching, preaching, but the thing that you must watch is their fruit, and also does their lifestyle line up with the Word of God? You can always tell a wolf by tracks, it is different from the flock. Don't just follow your pastor blindly because he could be a ravenous wolf awaiting someone's escape so that he can reel you back in. Today, its all about *"my members"*, or *"how many members do you have?"* we are all One Body friends aren't you thankful(Colossians 3:15)? Like let's say the Lord leads someone to Him through me, you there over in Georgia you gain as well! We are not separate bodies, nor communities but one. How has this happened my friends? How have we as the Church have gotten *so far* from our Father and Lord? Are we still living by Grace? Or is Mercy where we make our abode, because we don't want to truly follow the statutes of our Lord and King?

O children of God, ye chosen of God, ye called of God return ye back unto your Lord before the devourer devours your souls! Bring tithings and offerings unto the feet of God. Let your hearts revert back to the ways of the Christ, and let the ways of the devil leave your thoughts. No longer plan evil things against your brother, no longer wage war against your mothers and sisters. Allow God to manifest Himself unto you! You need teaching and you need the Grace of God to cover you! Come back unto the Father and hearken to His voice in which He speaks through His Son, Christ Jesus, for He is your God and Lord give Him your hearts, hearken back unto Him once again and you will receive Grace, Honor, Joy, Love, and Favor from your Lord and Savior Jesus Christ! Let Him be praised in the fields, in the land, in the sea, let all the earth praise Him Holy Name forever and ever, Amen. Selah. Hallelujah be to the One and True God, even, Jesus Christ, Who sits of the throne of His Father's Glory, Selah.

I pray these words over you that you may come out from battling your own! How many of you know and understand that there is an attack on the Church, and Satan has found his way into the Body of Christ? This is why we are attacking, hating,becoming jealous of one another, hating one another, and being able to hold grudges against your brother or sister. Our previous father whom we were delivered from, we have allowed back in, and we are willingly allowing him to do what he does, and that is *to kill, steal, and destroy!* I am upset that we have let such things happen, yet the Word of God prophecies *a great falling away*, but He also prophesies a *standard that shall rise up against the enemy.* Where is the standard friends? Why are we wanting to live like the world, dress like them, participate and partner with darkness? Why are our garments being blemished with sin? Haven't we been washed and cleansed by the blood of the Savior Jesus Christ? What we have been promised cannot be measured nor can it amount to the treasures, the blessings and the glory in heaven! God is our one hope and Who we have been reconciled to not back to Satan, the devil, why are we becoming materialistic like he is? *He doesn't savour the things of God, but rather the things of men(Mark 8:33, KJV)*. His concerns are of men, which are in other words the evil, carnal, materialistic things rather than the concerns of the Lord God, Who lives in the Spirit.

I see that many of us are becoming increasingly materialistic and carnal because when the Spirit is trying to move in the service, instead of participating in worship you are sitting! If some spoke of money and that you would receive it in two days you'd be up shouting like you already had it. What about *seeking first the kingdom of God*? Why are we becoming partners with our flesh again? We need to remain in the Spirit with the help of the Spirit of God. The reason you Holy Ghost seems dormant is because you are giving more room to flesh and feeding him rather than your spirit man. By Grace we were saved, by the Grace and Kindness of our Lord and Savior, why are we revoking the Grace of God now? Why are we looking more to our pastors as if they bled and died, and have all the answers rather than the Lord God of heaven? I say this humbly with all love and concern in my heart that many of you have fallen from the hands of Grace because of you willingness to want to sin right into the hands of Mercy. Those of you who hear the cry of the Father through my words I pray that ye repent, and be ye transformed back into the Image of the Living God that you may be a suitable sacrifice, a sweet smelling savor to the nostrils of our King.

If you have fallen as a saint you have the Grace of God to bring you back to His Favor by immediate repentance, as an unbeliever if you've never found Christ in God then you have Mercy from God to bring you unto you Grace and Favor through Obedience to Him. I can tell you my friends through countless sin that I have committed, I have tasted of Grace, Favor and Mercy. Through immediate repentance He has brought upon me His Grace, then by Obedience I was able to be clothed once again unto Favor, and lastly Mercy I have tasted of by sinning continuously when I promised Him

I would stop a certain sin, but through immediate repentance all I received by His Mercy was chastisement from Him! Praise God the Most High God, Who can counsel the Lord and show Him the Way to Wisdom, for He is it! Hallelujah! Thank Jesus the Christ for His powerful and mighty Right Hand that it is strong and makes way for Him. Amen. *Be strong in the Lord and His Spirit always never give any room nor any satisfaction to your flesh that you may continue to kill it by the sword of the Spirit which is God's Word, Amen*(Colossians 2:20-23).. I have one last scripture to bring before you eyes my brethren in Christ.

Romans 12:1-2,

¹I beseech you therefore, brethren, by the mercies of God, that ye present your bodies a living sacrifice, holy, acceptable unto God, which is your reasonable service.

² And be not conformed to this world: but be ye transformed by the renewing of your mind, that ye may prove what is that good, and acceptable, and perfect, will of God.

Start by repenting of your sins, calling on the name of the Lord, receiving power from His Spirit on High that you may fight the good fight of the faith, and hear those joyful words from the Lord. *"Well done, thou good and faithful servant thou hast been faithful over a few things, I will make thee ruler over many things: enter thou into the joy of thy Lord."* **Which** *is heaven. Be blessed in your going out, coming in, and in the field that you may give back unto the Father of Glory, Who sits on the throne of glory, Amen and Amen. Remain in Grace and Favor through Obedience to the King of Power that you may fear Him with all fear, and never fall from Grace into the hands of Mercy, Amen. Praise God.*

6. What can/do I do with all this Power and Knowledge?

       God is a *God of Wisdom*, and this power that *He* bestows upon *His people* is to those whom He chooses. What we must understand friends that not everyone in the world can be trusted with such power and knowledge only very few know such things in full what I have told you thus far. Many that have the knowledge don't know how to teach it correctly, because they are teaching not from the Holy Ghost. The Spirit of God has to recognize you in the Spirit in order to speak fluently through you without disturbances, just like He did His Son, Jesus Christ, and His disciples. As I said the our God is the God of Wisdom and as Him being the Lord, as King He rules by it and does not make a decision without it. Our God doesn't ever make a decision without including all of Himself, He doesn't halfway think things but thinks it all the way through even to the future in order to make a decision. You may be craving the Holy Ghost, with the power of tongues, but it may not be your time, or you are like Simon the sorcerer who only wanted the Holy Ghost for power and not the glorification of the Holy God.

       Do you think that you can bribe the Holy Ghost? Make a compromise with Him and trick Him? He is all knowing and as the Word of God He perceives hearts and minds from afar and knows the words on your tongue before you speak them. I adjure you my friends and understand my plea if you want the Holy Ghost, deny yourself: sinful desires, lust, wants, needs, cravings, be delivered from sin, no longer allow yourself to be tossed around by Satan doing his will but want to do the Lord's Will by taking a step of faith forward. When you take that step or leap of faith forward towards the King He will gladly take that step toward you as well. Now, don't think that you can hide from the face of the Lord, understand that He knows all things and His eyes are everywhere. Don't try to conjure up an evil plan along with the evil one to go against the Lord and His people for you will fail miserably. I say this so that by the Spirit of God that the hearts of those who are trying to enter the territory of the Christ and His sheep may not and fear the Lord with a great fear(and of course I say it in love from the Father of Heaven and Earth).

So going forward by the Holy Ghost I need you to understand what you are asking for, it is not just the power of God, but it *is* the power of God to *do His Will*. Also, it is the anointing and the grace to do such things that He requires(*you can also think of it as the stamp of approval from God to do the work that He has begun within you, Amen*). This is not something that you can receive then think that you don't have to do anything. Not so, because when you are given such power from on High by the God of all creation. You are immediately along with that given a task to spread the Gospel of the Lamb and His Sacrifice for humanity. With saying that, do not go before the Holy Ghost, but remain in His arms for further instruction. Because if you are not careful, the devourer can grab a hold of you if you are not careful, because you will not be in the will of God if you step before Him.

You are given this power as a boost to spread the word of God with power not in fear, because God has not given you a spirit of fear, but of power and of love(*which is the opposite of fear, not hate*). Our God is a God of power and preparation so with this power you are given, at first you are so ready to go out and go right into preaching, teaching, ministering, prophesying, healing, casting out demons, but as I stated He is a God of *Wisdom*. So we should allow ourselves to be lead by *His Wisdom*. Because if we are lead by our wisdom it will end it destruction and devastation. Moving forward, our God is a God of *Preparation and Perseverance* understand that He has everything under control, and since this is His Power running through your veins you must pay close attention to His voice that you go when He says *"Go."* I will show you some scripture when you go when the Lord has not permitted you to go to a place, and even though He did not permit you to go He will still be merciful toward you.

Jump over to Acts 21:10-11, 15-16, 27-30, 23:11. This speaks of Paul's ignorance toward the Holy Ghost by warning Him not to go Jerusalem, he was warned three times by the Holy Ghost; first through the mouth of the disciples by the Holy, secondly through his own prayer with those around Him, then again in prayer, and yet he still went. He ended being captured by the Jews of Asia thrown into prison, this was because God told him not to pursue his journey to Jerusalem. But the Lord shows Grace towards Paul, because of his testimony there in Jerusalem. And promises him an escape by saying, *"Be of good cheer, Paul: for as thou have testified of Me in Jerusalem, so must thou bear witness also at Rome."* So even though God knew that He was going to make that decision He showed Grace toward Paul, because even though he was bound in chains he still testified of the Great God and Lord and of His Great Power showed to Him, Amen.

I say unto you Spirit-filled saints please for the sake of Christ move by the Spirit of Christ that you may know where to go. Listen to His voice, whether it be through signs, visions, or your brethren be still in the presence of the Lord. For we need to move by the Holy One in these last and evil days, we must be very careful and highly vigilant because just as we are sent to spread the gospel there are those who are sent with the same kind of clothing as you, but are sent not to spread the gospel but to try and *constrain it*. Focus on the Lord of Hosts and you will never fail, follow in His statutes and I promise you that He will direct thy paths on the narrow path of leading to your glory which is Him(Are you excited? I am! To see my God face to face will be like no other!)!

This power that you were given is not to glorify your own self, but to glorify straightway God for He is the one who gave this to you. You are not of your own power but of the Holy Ghost, your Father my friends. Preach the gospel with power, authority, with all truth, and guidance from the Spirit of the Living God. Do not fear the anointing that is given unto you because you must recall that it is the Father *He doeth the works*. God told me, because I was once afraid of the anointing that I carry in the Holy Ghost, but just as His Son spake to the Pharisees when they rejected Him and blasphemed the Holy Ghost, that *"if ye believe not Me believe the works*(John 10:37-38)."* That He doeth the works not me so I needn't not be afraid of the people for I know that I am sent by the Lord to do His work as His servant not mine own servant nor by my own power will I do this, if so then I should be afraid. But I know who I am sent by and who I serve and His Name is Jesus the Christ the Holy One of God Who is my Father and Majesty! For I come bearing gifts and fruits that you may eat and consume by the Holy Ghost that you may be full with the knowledge of God and that you joy maybe full in Him. I am so excited to share with all of you the words and the concerns of God that you may know His heart and mind through my words. I am not any high priest, nor do I claim to be a prophet, pastor, not an apostle but I am a minister of the gospel for the Lord Jesus Christ that He may be glorified in me. Titles for me are null and void because I know who I am in Him I needn't not tell you for my works in the Lord will speak of themselves. If I tell you that I am a prophet, will you listen to me if I come to teach? If I say that I am a pastor or preacher will you listen to my words from the Most High if I prophecy? If I only go by the title of an evangelist will you count me unworthy and close your ears when I move in the way of an apostle? Regardless, this is not about me, but about the Savior and God, Jesus Christ, He is the One Who died on the cross and rose for your sins not me, but I am a servant of His by His Spirit.

I addressed the matter of titles for that is all we are about today in Church, *What title do you carry?* That shouldn't be the question, the question should be, *"Do ye carry the Holy Ghost of God within you?"* I will say this to you my friends many of you will get angry but how can you get angry at the truth if you abide in it? Some of us fear the titles that a person carries more than we fear God! Because someone claims to be a prophet you automatically think that they are moving by the Holy Ghost, and with that my friends they could prophesy anything and you'd believe it. Instead of believing the works of the person and looking at their fruits you look at their titles to dictate whether they be a person of God. Where are the watchmen for the Body of Christ friends? Where are you so called "prophets"? You prophecy peace when there is none, you prophecy blessings over a person while they are yet in sin. You prophecy rain when there is a drought coming upon the land. The true prophets are those of you who are not afraid to speak out and prophecy the things that the Church of today hates: punishment for sins, persecution, them being backslidden and what will come if they don't repent. Don't worry about the faces nor the words of those in the Church for they will only wished they listened to the voice of the prophet!

They will cry with a great shout, *"O Lord save us! Why do you persecute us with the sword and brimstone?! We have prophesied in Your Name, preached in Your Name, why are we in peril?"* And the Lord God of heaven will respond to you who block your ears with darkness, *" I have sent countless prophets among you to tell you of these things, but ye did not listen nor hearken unto My Voice; but you blocked it out with your pride and darkness, refraining from the Light. Yes, you have preached in My Name but I knew you not, for My Spirit does not recognize you because you are not of My Spirit but remained flesh, when I told you time and time again, bringing before you evidence of My Spirit and the knowledge of it that you might receive it and have Me dwelling on the inside of you. It is too late now, for you have made your choice, and I have made Mine," saith the Lord God of Hosts! Amen.*

God has brought before us, prophetically, His Word and what He will say to them at the time which is coming for you will cry out in despair for the God of heaven but His ear will not be open to you, nor will you be able to find His face. I say this not in joy, but in sorrow for I want not these things to happen to you, but it is not my lane to stop you, I can only tell you the word of the Lord and whatever you choose is between you and the Lord God of heaven, Amen, Praise God for His Wisdom and Power that has been given unto men, for I am grateful to have Him in my life and have Him forevermore, Amen and Amen.

The Lord God is very keen on us listening to Him, just as any father on earth is. Taking heed to the Lord's Word is the best way to receive His Favor, and to go far in Him(*faith included because without faith we cannot please God!*). *Trust in the Lord your God with all your heart, and lean not unto your own understanding(Proverbs 3:5, John 14:6) for He is the Way, the Truth, and the Life,* and He knows what's best for you and best of all where you are headed. Many of us start to build up in fear rather than love because sometimes we don't know where are headed, we even fear to trust God that He has it planned out. Trust me my friends, the Lord is faithful and sure to be there to guide you every step of the way! *For the steps of a good man are ordered by the LORD,(Psalm 37:23) and He delighteth in his way.* God takes delight in guiding you! *He would never guide you to a place that would harm you, for the thoughts in His mind toward you are peaceful and not of evil intent toward you*(Jeremiah 29:11)my friends, *trust in the God of Heaven* for He is Just and Upright therefore Faithful and Trustworthy! If you have the Holy Ghost of God within you, Who is God's own Spirit who searcheth the deepest things of God, and knows all I pray that you get in your Word and then you find God once again and have that connection with Him that you once had. Also, your prayer closet has been vacant so I hear God in the Spirit saying for you to *return to Him in your quiet place*, which is your place of prayer and the altar of worship in your home to Him.

Return, return, return my friends for God is speaking and He is speaking to those who will listen to Him, and there aren't many friends the question is, "*Are you one of them*?" You wonder why you brother is getting a Word and you aren't, then you heart is filled with indignation. Why? Because simply my brethren *you aren't in your closet to even get a Word from the Lord. Listen to His voice, and don't interrupt Him for His words are precious and there is Life and Light found in them also there are treasures forever more found in His Mouth. Praise God!* I wanted to take time by the Holy Ghost and break all of this down for you that you might have teaching from, and I say unto you that as I teach you God is teaching me also that I may be full in His Grace toward me, Amen.

So now that we understand the Holy Ghost and why He is given, and what the power is for we can now move forward, even deeper into the topic: *What can I do with this Power and Knowledge*? There are countless things that you must consider before you can began to question this. First you must understand who you are in the Spirit, you must seek the Spirit who knoweth the deeper things of the Living God that He may plainly reveal who you are called to be and what you are called to do for him. Ask God in the Holy Ghost during your prayers who you are, what office you are being called into. Are you a prophet, teacher, preacher, evangelist, an apostle? Even though I talked about I do not claim any titles it *is* important for *you to know* who you are not everyone else, but what I will say is that those who know you God will bring revelation/confirmation through them to you that you may know your place in the Kingdom of God. You can be prophetic without being a prophet, you can move in a apostolic way yet not be a full blown apostle it is *for you to seek and for you to find in the Lord*. Have you had dreams even since you were little, have you heard God's voice telling you things to come and they did but didn't know Who's voice it was? I want to specifically speak to the prophets by the Holy Ghost and you know who you are! Don't be afraid to accept this honorable office, yet even though it is a lonely road you must see the joy in it: *far from men, closer to God*!

Prophets are very peculiar and not liked among others, sometimes for no apparent reason. You know things before they happen, you are either a linguistic prophet in word who writes the Word of God when spoke to him/her, or a vocal prophet who speaks directly what the Lord is giving on the spot like many of the prophets back in the day(*see Samuel, Jeremiah, Daniel, even Jesus our Father who was the Master Prophet!*). You seemed to be *cast out from by the Church, even hated of them*, for you are the LORD's mouthpiece and the direct line to the Truth. Let this not hinder you from humbling yourself before the Lord that you may do what He has called you to do, because in this very hour that I write you we need you! Come on out! I as your brother embrace you in my arms in the Spirit that you may feel loved and not hated, if your blood brother hates you, know that you have a brother in the Spirit that loves you dearly and rejoices over you by the Spirit of God! God will vindicate you for those who have tried to mute your voice in the church. Wait, isn't the church built off of the foundation of the *prophets and the apostles*? So when they fight against you as the Church they are fighting against God my friends! *This is a warning to those of you who have done this to the prophets of today!* "*Touch not Mine anointed, and do My prophets no harm*", *saith the Lord*(*Psalm 105:15*)! If you are supposed to be an "anointed" man or woman of God and you try to sabotage and block another person's anointing you are in trouble! If you do not repent for you pride, competition, jealousy, and mishandling God's anointed and chosen ones *fire will be your end*. I say this to you out of love, for I wish that none of your perish! For God has called us to be One Body, and be thankful in Him, but some of us are getting big headed and are trying to grow your own head on the Body of Christ.

You are like a pimple that is offensive and unclean, God is about to use a strong ointment to remove you completely if you don't move back into the body through repentance my friends. For this is not about you, but this is about Jesus Christ why are we worried about ourselves? Why are we trying to promote our brand and not the brand of Christ Jesus?(*This is one of the reasons why I do not claim or go by any title that I may refrain from becoming big headed like you against Christ.*) I need you by the grace of God to allow yourselves to come back to your Lord, why have ye forsaken Him for vain imaginations and for evil in your hearts against your brothers and sisters in the body? *"Come back to Me, My Children, for I have much to do in you before such a time, if ye do not return fire and brimstone will be your dwelling place. I want this not for you, for it was never intended for you but for the devil, and his angels, but your lack of repentance and recompense toward Me is causing you to slip and fall back into sin, in which I have delivered you from,"* saith the God of the Heavens.

I come to cause your hearts to fear(*or highly respect*) the Lord with reverential trust, and hating evil and all that pertains to it, that you may no longer sow into the kingdom of Satan, but the glory of the kingdom of God friends. I have told ye what ye must do in order to find your way back to Him and how to find Him, repent, go back into your prayer/worship closet, back to the altar and call on the name of the Lord that He might save you from your sins! You may not like my speech but I am not at all ashamed nor fearful to speak the words of the Lord for He is My Strength and My Joy in the times of Battle, a Great Shield of Defense against the wiles of the enemy! For He is El Shaddai, *Elohim*, Jehovah Tsidkenu, Jehovah Jireh, Jehovah Nissi, Jehovah Rapha, Jehovah Shalom, Jehovah Adonai He is My Everything what can thou do against me and defeat me when I have the Lord? I boast not in myself, but in the

Lord of Hosts for His Arm is what fights for Him, and His Hand stretches out wide smiting my enemies far and wide, even if I have not knowledge of them. Isn't our God in Jesus Christ great?! He protects us from *seen and unseen danger, so follow Him.*

So *what can you do with this power? Or What do I do with this power?* Protect it, guard it with you heart by following the Lord Jesus our King in His footsteps! Don't allow the enemy to cause you to stumble, keep watch in prayer and by remaining in His Word! The more that you are in the Word and in the Spirit the more that you will be able to see the devices of the enemy working against you, my friends. Exercise the power of the Holy Ghost when needed(*as the Lord permits, don't go unless you feel lead*) as in praying over the sick, casting out demons, healing etc. Keep your focus on the Lord always bring everything that you learn from your pastors and/or elders bring it before the feet on the Master, the Holy Ghost who gives them the power to speak. Guard yourself in wisdom and knowledge that you may be able to know right from wrong when it pertains to the Word of God.

In order for your knowledge to increase in the word of God you must allow the Holy Ghost to teach you, for *no can teach you like the Holy Ghost can!* He is the Ultimate Teacher and knoweth all things that pertain to God, for He is the Spirit of Truth, also known as the Comforter and the Mighty God! He searcheth the deeper things of God look here at 1 Corinthians 2:9-13,

⁹ But as it is written, Eye hath not seen, nor ear heard, neither have entered into the heart of man, the things which God hath prepared for them that love him.

¹⁰ But God hath revealed them unto us by his Spirit: for the Spirit searcheth all things, yea, the deep things of God.

¹¹ For what man knoweth the things of a man, save the spirit of man which is in him? even so the things of God knoweth no man, but the Spirit of God.

¹² Now we have received, not the spirit of the world, but the spirit which is of God; that we might know the things that are freely given to us of God.

¹³ Which things also we speak, not in the words which man's

wisdom teacheth, but which the Holy Ghost teacheth; comparing spiritual things with spiritual.

I pray that receive this scripture for what is says, but for those who cannot quite grasp it this set of scriptures gives us a clear view of the Holy Ghost and that He is the Spirit of the Living God, of course making Him God. Now I explained to you how the Holy Ghost was God, the Christ before but just so you know that the term "ghost" is meant to be put in the category of someone that is deceased. There for when Christ *the Soul or Man* of God came and when He *"deceased"* He then represented Himself as next the Holy Ghost, showing Himself as the Living Spirit of God conquering death and its grip! Therefore making the work of the Father, the Son complete now God has to show the role of the Holy Ghost, the Spirit of the Living God and making an abode in us as His Home or Temple. Teaching us the ways of His Son and Himself through the power of the Holy Ghost by having His thoughts in ours that *we may become one just as He and His Father are indeed one. Amen!*

God has given His Precious Spirit to those who He has *chosen*, therefore this *needs* to be known that God is NOT going to give His Spirit to just anyone. He knows the hearts of men, and their intentions as *for He is the Word of God(see Hebrews 4:12-14).* It is His job to protect the anointing, His power and His Word for those of you who have received the Lord's Spirit, rejoice! I say again unto you, *"Rejoice!" in the Lord always(Philippians 4:4).* For you have been *chosen* by *the Most High God to carry the anointing of the Lord Jesus to carry out His Work here on Earth!* Aren't you excited? When you have the Holy Ghost your joy never runs out! Why? Because *He is our source of Joy and our source of Power! Look here at the Words of the Holy Ghost Himself, These things have I spoken unto you, that my joy might remain in you, and that your joy might be full(John 15:11).*

Therefore, going forward, Jesus is the Teacher and you must have a teachable spirit! This is what the Lord is looking for that He may have an open vessel to *teach through and to allow Him to have His Way.* God promised His Holy Ghost to come upon the young and the old in these last and evil days, but to those whom He has chosen. If ye are tarrying for the Holy Ghost continue tarrying for His Spirit to be within you, continue believing for Him to reign His power over you and in you. It may just be that you need a breakthrough to the Holy Ghost, *I pray these words over you by the Holy Ghost,(the Lord promised me that if ye pray the words that I am about to put before you those of you who are tarrying for His Ghost ye shall receive! Believe in the word of God not mine! For the words I pray are of His Spirit not mine own for He groaneth things that we men cannot understand unless He maketh it plain in the way we can understand what He saith to His children.) Pray this, O God of Heaven, You Art the One Who was and Who is. You are the El Shaddai, Elohim, for I have listened and hearkened my ear unto the servant of the Lord for His Words are your and I see them for I believe in saying these words that I will receive your Holy Ghost! O Lord reign down Your Fire from Heaven upon me! Reign down your power to cast out demons, heal the sick and the lame, to testify before governors and government leaders just as You promised O God, for You are indeed the King and God of Promises. For you lead the children out of the land of Egypt and out of the hands of Pharaoh through the Red Sea by Your Promise. Give me O God your power that I may do thy work here on earth not to glorify myself but to glorify You O, My God. For thou art Holy, thou art Righteous, and thou art Powerful, thou art the Holy One of Israel, Your Son, Christ Jesus, who is also known as the Holy Ghost. I have understood the demands and teachings of Your servant and I bow to You O God that I may receive you into my bosom, Amen. And as the words of our Lord say, Receive ye the Holy Ghost.*

Many of you shall receive the power of the Holy Ghost for the Father has promised me that and I shall meet some of you(for I saw some of you in a vision receiving Him from reading the words and I say to you that no matter where you are let the praises ring out! Let the tongues flow through you that you receive in full the Holy Ghost as the Lord shows us His Power in Acts 2:3-5.)! Rejoice! Rejoice in the Lord for you have receive the tongues of heaven, you have reached the "last" step of salvation going through the fire of the Holy Ghost that you may become clear as glass filled with the power of His Spirit! For I may not see you now, but I rejoice with you in the Lord in Spirit that His Will was done and it will continue to be in our lives for He that started a work in us is surely faithful and willing to complete it in the name of the Lord Jesus Christ! Amen, Selah! Remember no tongues, no Holy Ghost.

With saying that, I heard the Lord say unto me after I had written this and prayed as He ask to talk about and address *the counterfeit* as He put it. He literally said, *"Talk about the counterfeit." And so I shall Lord Jesus!* We all know that the Lord Jesus Christ is the source of all that is good, and then there is the antichrist, the devil, who is the source of all things evil(*which is sin*). The devil in the Bible counterfeits, or *makes a fake copy* of the things of God. Don't believe me? Go to Exodus,*(you know that I always will have scripture by the Holy Spirit because He leads me, I cannot lead my own self or less I'd be lost!) 7:8-12,*

⁸ And the LORD spake unto Moses and unto Aaron, saying,

⁹ When Pharaoh shall speak unto you, saying, Shew a miracle for you: then thou shalt say unto Aaron, Take thy rod, and cast it before Pharaoh, and it shall become a serpent.

¹⁰ And Moses and Aaron went in unto Pharaoh, and they did so as the LORD had commanded: and Aaron cast down his rod before Pharaoh, and before his servants, and it became a serpent.

¹¹ Then Pharaoh also called the wise men and the sorcerers: now the magicians of Egypt, they also did in like manner with their enchantments.

¹² For they cast down every man his rod, and they became serpents: but Aaron's rod swallowed up their rods.

For Satan always tried to copycat or counterfeit my God, it's really funny honestly, but anyhow they immediately went to work to topple over what Moses had done. All of their rods became serpents(this kind of power can only be give from God, Satan does not have this power, just as he will have been given power by God to deceive by reigning fire from heaven, but the power is *never his own.*) but to show that God has the power Aaron's one staff swallowed theirs. The Lord showed me this in His Spirit as I was typing that look the power came from God for all of them to do it, correct? So in saying that to show who has the true power of the Lord Jesus inside of them He cause the rods of the magicians to be swallowed and return back to Aaron. *This is why*

Pharaoh's heart was hardened against the Lord because He was showing that He was the God of the world in Moses and Aaron, and not him. Whew! Our God is One Mighty God!!

I brought these set of scripture before your eyes that you may see and understand this(*with saying that some of you may have already caught on to what I am about to say in the Holy Ghost*) that yes, Satan has tried to copy the Holy Ghost in tongues! This is why many of you *"prefer"* to *not* speak in tongues because you think that they are all demonic! Well, let me say this to you my friends you need the Holy Ghost and the *only way that you can receive Him and know that you have Him is the evidence of tongues.* By saying that, Satan has deceived you and had carried out His plan(s) first: to get you to doubt the word of God(Acts 2:3-5); secondly: to deny the power of God; and thirdly: therefore moving without God, the Holy Ghost! This is what he *wants!* Don't allow him to block you from the true knowledge of God the Holy Ghost! How can you tell if they have His Spirit or not? By the Spirit of God, by their *fruits*! Do they exude Christ? Is their conversation of the holies? How is their conversation concerning Christ, do they give Him Glory? Can they say His Name? Can they say that He is the Son of God, and that He came in the flesh and continues to still come in the flesh today?

God just brought this to my attention, Is there walking and lifestyle lining up with His? If not even one of these matches, you may one to pray and question rather if they have true Holy Ghost that Jesus baptizes His people in. How do you know you have the Holy Ghost? In the same fashion those around you have the Holy Ghost their Spirit will connect with yours if not there's something up. Look at it like this if there are three minds agreeing in the Spirit of the Living God and one is on a different page there is a problem! Either those three are not of the *Holy Ghost* or you are of another spirit! I pray that ye have no confusion! In the name of the Lord Jesus Christ for He is not the author of confusion, but of peace and joy(*1 Corinthians 14:33*) Ultimately God shall be the judge of it, and *He shall direct thy paths if thee be a good man*, but if ye are not of the goodness of Christ then your roads leads to destruction and brimstone!

For by the goodness of Christ I have taught you, more in depth of the *Holy Ghost by the Holy Ghost* and what to watch out for! For as I say God has His heavenly tongue and the devil, that is Satan has his demonic tongue. For witches, warlocks, all those who oppose Christ and who are full of the spirit of the antichrist, yet claim to have the Holy Ghost have their own tongue! For there is and will always be a drastic difference in tongues, the tone and the sound of it will be drastically different. When you are in the Spirit and someone else speaks in the language of the Spirit it should only elevate the service/prayer, however, if a witch comes in speaking her language and you don't feel a shift but rather a heaviness in the Spirit, or a downpull, that isn't God! For there are those of you who are bold! You sit and listen to the tongues of others and try to *counterfeit* their tongues, *just as your father, the devil does.* For you have been spotted and the Lord sees you, think not that you can hide for the eyes of the Lord are everywhere! For *Proverbs 13:5* states and I quote,

> *3 The eyes of the LORD are in every place, beholding the evil and the good.*

For He hath created thee and has the right to this for He is Holy and Just, not perverted, not invasive of privacy, but *only observes to record the doings of the good and evil that they may stand before the judgement seat of Christ and be judged.(2 Corinthians 5:10)Amen.*

So God has given you this power to be of a great witness of Him and of His Power, to be a reservoir it and an ambassador of Christ that you may carry out the divine plan following His Holy steps leading to our Glory which *is Him, Hallelujah Amen!!* For our King wants to teach you of His Way while Him being inside of you, you having His mindset. As the scriptures in 1 Corinthians stated *how can a spirit know the things of a man, save it be his own spirit?* I believe, by the Holy Ghost that He uses this also to say this, *'How can we know the deeper things of God if we not have His Spirit in us?'* For see it like this friends I can explain to you in word of a particular thing that I am speaking of, but rather for you to *truly* understand what I see in my mind, feel in *my spirit.* Well, you would have to have my exact mind! So, we see the Genius of our God here in this context He is literally showing us His Master plan that He had concocted before any of us existed. That He knew in order for us to follow His statutes to a tee, we would need to have His Spirit and mind place within us so that we may know *the deeper things of God.* Without Him within us we cannot teach the word of God the way that we are supposed to, and how God sees fit. Therefore because those of you who don't have the Holy Ghost, but you have God on the outside or rather the surface that is all your going to get is *surface knowledge.* For those of us that have the Spirit of the Living God, we get the *deeper knowledge of God because we have Him within us.* See the difference? *Philippians 2:5-6,*

> ⁵ *Let this mind be in you, which was also in Christ Jesus:*
> ⁶ *Who, being in the form of God, thought it not robbery to be equal with God.*
> *(Jesus Christ was and is and has always been the mind of God the Spirit, as a prerequisite of the intimacy that we would share with Christ our God!)*

If you are believers of God, then why are you deniers of the power of God through tongues? You make you way through Bible college yet come out still not quite understanding the power of God nor the Oneness of Him, His soul and Spirit(God the Father, Son, and Holy Ghost). You have been pastoring for over fifty years and still haven't tasted of the power of the Holy Ghost! People will say, *"Well, that is their opinion,"* or *"That's what they chose to believe".* Now I understand if you were brought up denying the power of the Holy Ghost because those who taught you did the same, but, however, I am speaking to those of you that have been in church and in the Word of God for a *very long time.* Your knowledge of the truth is what is keeping your church from growing *because you are not willing grow yourself as the leader of your church.* I pray ye don't be like the Pharisees and *shut up heaven for those who need to access it, then on top of then ye do not go in yourselves.* My heart is saddened at this! Your unwillingness to comply with the God Who *created you and Whom you are supposed to serve!* You have changed the truth of God into a lie, crafting and devising you own selfish doctrine to rather uplift yourselves rather than the God of heaven, Jesus Christ, Himself. Your doctrine speaks as you as the head of the Body rather than Christ, it says that they are to bring tithes, offerings, and other sacrifices to *your* feet rather than *the feet of Christ Jesus the Savior!*

Are you God the Savior? Did you die for my sin? Is the blood stained banner yours? Oh, let me worship you then! That's unthinkable! You are just a man liken unto me, and Christ was much more than you are now. He was both man and God at the same time conquering death and hell for us that we may go forward into Life with Him! Can your name save me and wash me clean? Make me whole? I think not! For there is *one God, and one that is True and His Holy and Matchless Name is Christ Jesus.* Understand this that you have been seen and noticed by the eyes of the Savior and those of you who are wolves in sheep's clothing prepare yourself for a *rude awakening if you are not willing to leave the flock. I speak to you evil spirits who have manifested yourselves in them, for you are ravenous and evil, the Lord has already defeated you for you will be forever under His feet. Now, I speak to the hearts of the men and women that have been sent to be deceivers of the Gospel, to try to pervert it be better if you tied a milestone to your neck and jumped into the ocean for you are perverting the flock therefore touching and trying to grasp in the hands of the Lord! Your days are coming to an end, and they shall come sooner than you think! Once you've read this your clock will be ticking, make a choice now!*

For the Lord saith unto you, " *For I AM the God of both heaven and earth; fear Me! for I have clothed the earth and all its majesty. I have given it it's splendor, I AM also the One who waters her gardens, and trims away the weeds and thorns! For in my eyes you are a thorn, and I shall cast you out into outer darkness that you may no longer be in My sight. I am prolonging this season for your salvation, but it isn't long until I reign down My fury upon My enemies. Will you be My friend or My foe? I reach out to you as both Father and Creator in saying: 'Take My hand for I AM the Lord thy God, the Christ Who died and rose from the grave for you.' You cannot hide from for My eyes are everywhere and I have known you before the foundation of the earth, never has a man seen Me, but I have seen thee and know thee. Hearken unto My call before time has ended for My watch is drawing closer and closer to the day of terror, and the day of Redemption for My saints that abide in Me. The day of terror will either be your fate and destruction or My Glory shall be your story. Hearken unto Me for My Love burns for you day and night and I groan for your heart to be Mine once again. I call to you, awaiting your answer that I may rejoice in song and dance that my beloved hath finally returned to Me,"* saith the Lord thy God of heaven and earth, Jesus, the Christ the Messiah and Savior of the world!!!

At my closing of this chapter I want to reiterate something by the Holy One that not *all* can be apostles, prophets, evangelists, preachers or teachers my friends, but the Lord Jesus by His *Ghost* has only called *some*. Look here in scripture that you may fear the Lord;

Ephesians 4:9-15,

⁹ (Now that he ascended, what is it but that he also descended first into the lower parts of the earth?

¹⁰ He that descended is the same also that ascended up far above all heavens, that he might fill all things.)

¹¹ And he gave some, apostles; and some, prophets; and some, evangelists; and some, pastors and teachers;

¹² For the perfecting of the saints, for the work of the ministry, for the edifying of the body of Christ:

¹³ Till we all come in the unity of the faith, and of the knowledge of the Son of God, unto a perfect man, unto the measure of the stature of the fulness of Christ:

¹⁴ That we henceforth be no more children, tossed to and fro, and carried about with every wind of doctrine, by the sleight of men, and cunning craftiness, whereby they lie in wait to deceive;

¹⁵ But speaking the truth in love, may grow up into him in all things, which is the head, even Christ:

God gave us the gifts to measure up to Himself, because we must realize that God when He came on the earth He was all of these gifts in one; a Teacher(Rabbi), a Mighty Master Prophet(prophesied more than a millenia into the future and lo, all the events which He hath spoken are coming to pass in His Name), He evangelized, outreached to the people through the Gospel of Himself healing, teaching and ministering to those who were sick and in need, as a pastor or The Great Shepherd He reminded the Pharisees of the law while teaching the disciples He also preached the Word into their hearts that they might not do opposite to His Word, and of course He taught the Pharisees through love their wrongs, and all those who followed Him taught them the True Gospel of God *teaching them the deeper things of God.* If Christ is the *Head of all things* this makes Him God, being above all things? This is surely God in Himself showing His love by giving us these gifts, and with saying that *no one* and I mean *no one* can choose their own office! It has to be given from Spirit by the Spirit! You cannot be a prophet, teacher, or anything that is listed without going through the fire of the Spirit, the Holy Ghost!

How can you be a prophet, yet you are still blind? How can you preach without have been taught? How can you be in a place of apostleship and leadership, and be lost yourself? There is no way to harness these gifts without the Spirit! Don't you see? God gave us these gifts that we may not be above the body, but be servants and ministers, even tend to the body if you will by teaching, loving, leading by the Holy Ghost! God gave me a vision in my sleep of two men, one represented a living sacrifice for he was upon a rock and I was the other man praying over Him asking the Lord to reign fire upon this man that He may be filled with the Spirit of God. I lifted my hands up in the air and God did so, but then the dream switched, while I was in the process of doing so, I saw a pool of lava(which represented the fire of God, the anointing which is the Holy Ghost) and there were different things in the pool. God spoke to me in the dream teaching me that each item represented an office, but one that really stood out to me was a human eyeball. He spoke to me after the vision and said that it represented the seers, the office of the prophet, and in my dream I saw pastors giving these offices to people(and these people were people who haven't been baptized with fire.). They used a spoon to scoop out the eyeballs and gave it to men and women. At the beginning of the dream I shouted and said by the Holy Ghost, *"You cannot possibly think that you can become a prophet without the fire!"*

So my question to you "*in the gospel*" who called you to be a prophet? Who called you to be a pastor? If you have not been through the fire of God? This is not a matter of preference! This is about truth and whom you serve! God is not the author of confusion, but of peace! Who are you? Your pastors have given you these titles! They sat and judged you in their offices and called you to be a prophet! God has not appointed you but your pastor has so therefore you are his prophet not God's. Your prophecies are empty with no truth, for they are approved by men rather than God, you seek to please man, and humble yourself to them rather than your King. I am calling you out by the Holy Ghost for you have done much damage and evil, your hearts are full of darkness and cruelty. None of your "prophecies" have come to pass, your prophecy a new home within three years those years pass but that person returns to you for answers but you brush it off by saying, " If you are faithful over a few things, God will make you ruler over many!" You quote scripture yet there is no Word in you, neither is there life in you. False prophets! God sees you and knows you, you say that you come in the name of the Lord yet you do not understand His Ways nor move by them. You move to the right and God is saying to move to the left! You are the opposite of truth and if you aren't careful your own prophecies will be your own downfall. You will only be able to blame yourself, for God warned yet you still remained in your lies and evil. Don't think you pastors who named your congregant something that he isn't that you will not suffer for your wickedness, for the damage that they have done is only a baby to what you have done to the people of God! God holds you responsible for these crimes, for they were under your tutelage and He will judge you justly for your doings!

The Holy Ghost will make known who you are my friends, and He will make it very, very clear. For if *He* called you then you are already His, seek Him that He may be found by you and that you may know your identity in the Lord Jesus! *May God be praised forever and ever, and may His Glory be shown in us as we follow His Holy Will! Amen!*

7. Prophets of Today

Brothers and sisters of *the Spirit of prophecy of the Lord Jesus Christ* I come unto you in the name of the Lord Jesus to bring you gifts of knowledge and the benefits of warning. Your job in the kingdom of God is not only to tell the people of the future events to come, but also to warn and remind them of the darker things that are upon us(*be not afraid to do this for the Lord will be with you, for you shall speak His Words*). If you are a prophet then you know what *Spirit*, I am of, I say this with much confidence because the Father hath sent me to you through word to give this to you and as you are reading this your spirit is taking witness of these words because He hath given them to me.

There is much to do in the Kingdom, and the labourers are few, you as the chosen prophets of God are called to seek out those who are called by the Living God that you may bring them into the Kingdom of God *by His Hand.* I ask that you open your eyes even deeper into the Spirit that you may receive all of these words that I am about to write unto you from our Father Jesus Christ. This is what He saith now unto you,

" *I am sending word unto you My prophets through My son, Jordan, that He may lay upon you the gift in which you've been seeking and that is an okay to go. To commence your ministry in prophecy! I have given many of you assignments already in what you must do before I return yet you seem to be stagnant in your walk with Me. Listen not to the enemy or those around you, you know what I have spoken unto you concerning your ministry let Me help you to start. You need no one but Me, for there is none that can take care of you the way that is needed. Many dreams, signs, and visions have been given unto you My prophets, display them before the Church that they may fear My Name once again and return back to Me. You are My Mouthpieces open your mouth so that My Words may flow off of your tongue," saith the Father of Heaven, " I send you out now to do what I have called thee to do and that is prophecy, heal, set free, break chains off of your fellow brothers and sisters, and to bring back what the enemy has stolen, what the Church has allowed him to steal and that is order! Chaos runs through the church like a river and there is no Rock to stop the flow. For they have removed Me and have place Me to the side that they may be glorified and receive the praises from men and the Church. Corruption is there and you know this because I hath shown you, you know who you are. Look not unto the wickedness of this world, but unto the glory that shall be revealed and discovered once you reach heaven with Me," saith the Lord Jesus the Christ, Who is the Father, and the Son, and the Holy Ghost, the Holy One of God, Amen! Selah.*

Prophecy prophets! Do what you were called to do! Our God is giving the thumbs up! The green light in order for you to begin what He has called you to do my fellow brothers and sisters. God is pleased with your hearts, and for your patience with Him, allow Him to open your mind as the prophet to the possibilities of God that you may have faith in full in all things. I want you to know that God is raising you up to greater heights, to greater things that you may do what He has called you to do, to bring you before men that you may prophecy and do mighty works for His Glory by *His Hand.* All the pain that you have suffered for the greater good, trust me it was worth it and God will raise you up in due time. You will look back and say, *"I was there, and look where I am now!"*

You know what God has spoken unto you act when He says for you to act! For He shall guide you and protect you in everything that you do. For in Jesus Name shall you do these things, and present will He be in Jesus Name, Amen.

Beware of the false prophets for they will try to blend in among you that they may get some sort of credit, or may even be bold enough to try to damage and uproot your gift. Don't allow this to happen for the Lord God hath called thee, and power has He given you that you may trample over lions, scorpions, and dragons. Use this power by faith to rebuke and reprove them from you, that they may fear the name of the Lord Jesus Christ our Heavenly Father. God has shown me a vision that they too have been sent out, but they are sent out to destroy, be very careful for Satan is cunning and just when you think that that person is on your side they turn and bite you like a snake! Let not their scales hypnotize you, but when you see this go the other way! If the Father hath not given you the power nor the authority or the grace in order to deal with something in this case it is best to be quiet and let the Lord Jesus handle the situation. Your words do not match His, so let the Lord do His Wondrous work that He does.

Understand this, my friends, that you have been called to a great work as a prophet that you may claim and take back what the enemy has stolen from God people! You are the mouthpieces of God, so your ear is at His Mouth that you may speak unto the people, just like our brothers

Moses, Elijah, Samuel and the other prophets hath done. They are not above us but they are our brothers and sisters just like you and I are brothers/sisters. They have paved the way for us twenty-first century prophets. For those of you who bare the spirit of prophecy, you know that you are of old, for this Spirit was before the world began just the Lord Himself spoke over the prophet Jeremiah. And since you are of old, you must understand your role. That we are dealing with ancient, old demons, so like you we have to have those who are *of old* in order to deal with these things. *Does that make sense?* As prophets, you are sent to bring order in the Church and this is why the enemy hates you so, because just like the Lord you see straight through to the root of the issue, and not the flower, nor the stem, but the *root, the source of the problem in the body.* For you uncover the tactics of the enemy before they are even started, you see straight to the evil that is being plotted against the herd, or yourself. God has given you insight on the deeper knowledge of God that you may walk in His Holy Kingly statutes that you may bring order back to the house of God, because you are *in order with the Holy Ghost yourself!*

Remember as prophets of God, you bring the word of God before the people, and you must understand that everything that God gives is given unto the vessel *first*, so that you may be in order with God. Never think that you are above anyone just because you are bringing the prophetic word of God to the people! God will sit you down at the snap of a finger, for this position not everyone can attain to it my friends, for you have been chosen, *handpicked by the Father Himself.* Isn't it amazing to know that you are chosen by the King of kings to serve a key role in His *Kingdom*? Rejoice! For you have been found worthy by the Lord's Grace to be a prophetic voice *in the Lord Jesus Christ*!

7.1 Spiritual Boundaries

As being prophets of today you must remember our boundaries, who you are and what you are sent to do. Many don't like to hear nor read about minor prophets. Why? Because you that could be you, you need to go repent, and get your heart right with the Lord. Humble yourself before

Him. Why do I say these things? Because I see your hearts that you want a bigger title and want to bring glory to yourself! You think that you are something for having the title as the prophet, but one thing that you failed to realize is that the higher the position the more humble you must be before the Lord! There is no room for self-glorification, pride or arrogance. God being the Master Prophet, when He came He completely humbled Himself. Stripping Himself of *visible glory* that we might behold Him in Human form. And not only that Jesus came and *served* rather being the one being *served to.* Isn't that awesome of our God to do such things? Yes. For He, the Lord Jesus Christ is gracefully kind! His Love is never ending nor is it limited. Glory to Jesus our God and Holy King!

What you must understand is that a prophet is sent forth to declare and to remind God's people of His Works, to warn, to bring order back to the house of God, speak directly the King's Words to His sheep, to claim back territory, and to bring forth gifts to the people(both physical and spiritual). He/she is to unlock the spiritual door to all knowledge by the Hand of God and disperse it unto his/her fellowservants in Christ. So you see the depth and the weight of this office my friends, and how much of an impact that you all have as "second in command" in the Body of Christ after the apostle! This is why you must be very careful where you go and who you allow ourselves to be around because if not we can step out of the will of God if we are not aware. With saying that now let's dive right on in to *boundaries in the Spirit* since we are discussing stepping out of the will of God, and doing things outside of what He has given you the grace to do. First off as prophets whether you be a minor prophet or a major prophet in the Spirit, you *still* have a large impact in the spiritual world. Don't think that you aren't doing anything that you are not reaching anyone because you are! Another problem that I see second to self-glorification is that you have the wrong mindset, you are thinking carnally and *not* spiritually as you should as a prophet. Because we must remember that all of our work is done by the Spirit in the Spirit for the benefactory of the Spirit. So thinking that it is more important to have a physical impact is totally wrong and you are in error because your authority is given unto you by the Spirit of God, and you are called to come against the spiritual wickedness of this world yet if you only think about a fleshly impact you will fail greatly because you have no spiritual authority(or at least you haven't accessed it like you need to) and therefore have no power. Therefore these demons will take you over if you are not careful, deception could set in and you wouldn't be aware of it because you spiritual eyesight is locked up when God has given you the key to unlock it(*Prayer, worship, and praise!*).

You major prophets or *prophets to the nations* have a national or international anointing to reach the whole country(*wherever you are in the world*). Your ministry is not only local, but global your prophetic voice is to be heard all in the earth being an echo-chamber for the Holy Ghost to speak within and through you as His Prophet. You have been given a great mantle of an anointing that not many can say they have for prophets such as this *truly* need to be at the Hip of the Father, and have your ear pressed up against His Mouth. Because you will be reaching thousands to millions even billions of people for the sake of the Father and the glorification of His Son! Be ye grateful and understand that you have been hand selected, chosen for such a time as this to bring forth the Kingdom of God once again on the earth and the power thereof, Amen. So it's important to know you boundaries, with saying that just because you may be a major prophet does not mean that you are meant to go outside of your country. Remember evil is always awaiting you! Don't go beyond your limits, because where there is no grace there is no coverage and no coverage no protection my friends! That's why it is ***so important that you humble yourself before the Lord!*** Because where there is pride and arrogance there is disobedience and where there is disobedience there is rebellion, then you will find yourself pumping yourself up then you do what the Lord warned you not to do them a demon meets you on the other side! What then? All that false confidence that you had burns away because you realized that you went without the most important person, God the Lord Jesus, leaving you without power and grace to do anything. I adjure you friends take these things to heart, don't snicker or get an attitude, because the Lord God is watching and so respond wisely. If you are so offended that you choose not to read this book again then you can't follow God, and what I mean by that is that God is a God of Truth, He is it and He dwells in it if you can't accept the Truth then you don't accept Him, simple as that.

Now going on to you minor prophets, just because you don't go outside of your city limits doesn't mean that you aren't making an impact! Look at our brother Zechariah, he prophesied the return of our Savior, also gave a message of hope and faith for the Jews. His ministry was 2 years bringing forth detailed prophecies of the advents of the coming Christ! And you see how short his ministry was yet he was used in *such* a mighty and powerful way by the Lord revealing His Glory before his eyes in visions, and descriptive words from His Mouth. So you see that whomever the Lord chooses for His Glory, He will use in a very strong and impactful way, it doesn't matter who they were called to be! Get your heads out of the clouds, stop seeing things narrow mindedly and see in the Spirit that *God has chosen you!* Quit seeing things in a carnal and fleshly way, you want to be seen before the eyes of men, and I am telling you you need to rethink your priorities, wants and desires and as the prophet of God align them with His. Know this *God will be glorified, and you will be satisfied.* Why because Jesus spoke and said, *"Better is it to give than to receive."* Giving God control is the best feeling in the world, seeing Him be the One Glorified is awesome and trust me it *will* leave you breathless. He not only should be glorified, but *deserves to be glorified.* For all that He has done for you and for me there should be *no* competition between you and Him being glorified, that is why I say and so does the Lord, *"Humble yourself before the Lord thy God."* Flesh(*or sin*) cannot be glorified, or it cannot be seen as good because it is evil and the opposite of God and His Holiness.

Boundaries, boundaries, boundaries remain within them wherever the Lord has placed you, we all need you no matter what you were called to do whether it be to serve as a deacon, a healer, a pastor, prophet, evangelist, apostle, teacher and every little thing in between know that you are important to the body of Christ. Without you can the rest of the body function? If the blood is not pumping correctly to the feet of the body could be walk? Nope, so stay within what you are called and chosen so that we may all work accordingly for the glorification of the Lord the Godhead, Amen.

7.2 Spiritual awareness & sensitivity

God has given you *His Spirit* in order to do and complete the things that be of the *Spirit*, so you need to make sure that you are *spiritually aware* of all things that pertain to which you were called. Jesus tells us to have a teachable spirit because it pleases Him and allows Him to have His way through and within us. Therefore when we have a teachable spirit what next should come along with that is a sensitive spirit to the Spirit as in being attentive like the antennas to a t.v. when the antenas moves the t.v. automatically changes with the antena. Be the t.v. change and do as the Lord wants you to so that glorification may come to His Holy Name. God is the Lord and He wishes to see you as He sees and that is from a High standpoint or mindset, so no matter what you are called to see as the Lord sees and think of yourself *Highly in Him*, because when He thinks of you He thinks *Highly of you, because He is the Most High the Highest of High, Amen.*

Be ye sensitive to the Holy Ghost so that He can have His Way on this earth. Always have your ear right next His mouth and as He speaks you speak, as He moves so do you. Hallelujah, Amen!

7.3 Spiritual confidence in Christ

Christ being the Holy Ghost gave us these gifts that they benefit and keep His body that is forming underneath Him. Be confident in knowing that He called you, you sure didn't call yourself so you know that you have all the approval you need as a prophet of God because you were chosen by the One Who holds the Highest position in the earth and above in the heavens. Let no one tell you otherwise, just because they don't like what you have to say doesn't mean that you are not who God has called you to be. You aren't limited by what men say or do, you don't need men's approval of you like I said before you were *chosen by the Highest of High* not by yourself nor men, but by the hand of Christ *alone*. God is greatly to be praised!

Go forth doing the work of the Lord as a faithful and confidence soldier in the *Lord Jesus Christ*. Don't worry about the look on their faces, what they shout at you, you are *called and chosen remember?* Always have what the Lord thinks of you and what He has said about you in you mind and heart so when persecution comes(*and it will surely come*) you will be able to *stand your ground in confidence in the Spirit of the Lord and in Him alone* using your shield of faith against your enemies, Amen. God be praised for such wisdom and grace for such words and teaching. Hallelujah, Amen and Amen! Praise God the Lord Jesus!

Remember what the Lord said, *"My yoke is easy, and My burden in light."* Take upon the weights and "stresses" of the Lord for He is never fearful, defeated, and is always in a place of Joy. He wants you to *cast all cares upon Him for He careth for you.* Allow Him to strip *all fear of men* from you that you may go with the fire of the Lord burning up your enemies and destroying all what they've built and rebuilding what they have destroyed. Be ye progressive in the Holy Ghost, that you are constantly putting faith toward Him in all situations no matter what it may be. For He is surely Trustworthy and has *never told a lie nor has He repented, ever.*

Just so that you have the scripture(*Matthew 11:28-30*)right here before your eyes so that if you are struggling with this that you may overcome by reading His Words to you, how much He cares for you, and how much He is willing to do anything for His children.

28 Come unto me, all ye that labour and are heavy laden, and I will give you rest.

29 Take my yoke upon you, and learn of me; for I am meek and lowly in heart: and ye shall find rest unto your souls.

30 For my yoke is easy, and my burden is light.

God is awaiting your exchange my friends, *exchange fear for His Love and burdens, Amen. Praise God the Most High King!*

7.4 Knowing that God can pull you out of any situation

God will not give you any more than you can bear friends, for He is not a taskmaster that tells you to do this and doesn't offer to help. He is always there to assist you, an *ever present help in times of trouble.* Know that He can and will pull you out before it is too late, that He always has a contingency plan to get you out. Have faith in Him my friends, especially you prophets for you go forth proclaiming the things of heaven to men, to those who are full of darkness and surrounded by it, you allow God to bring Light to those men. So trust in Him that He will be there whenever you need help, and that when things go wrong He can pull you out just as He did when the evil hands of the Pharisees tried to grab a hold of Him. If *He* can get *Himself* out of a multitude of people, *He* can surely do it for you!

> [39] *Therefore they sought again to take him: but he escaped out of their hand.(John 10:39). Amen.*

Give God praise for we are never alone, for He is always with us even in times of trouble, as our Friend guides us by faith towards the heavenly goal in Christ. Thank God for His amazing Grace!

7.5 Rebukes & Rebuttals

As a prophet as I said by the Lord that you are sent to set order in the house of God, bring forth the words of the King *just* as He speaks. So with this many people are not going to agree, and many will get angry at you and hate the work that you are doing for the Lord(*even those in the church, so be aware of your surroundings*). Jealousy and sabotage will try to arise but the King of Glory will make sure to it that you come out on top, *for He is above all things and He hath called you above all things, because He thinks Highly of you.* He didn't make sure of what the men thought of you before He called you. Be who you are and be pleased of it in the Lord! In these last days not only are you prophets called to *rebuke and reprove* but all those whom the Lord sees fit whether you be a pastor, or whomever He chooses at that time. Now, when you bring rebukes open make sure that you are being lead by the Lord and that you were given the Grace to do so after following what He has set for you to do prior to doing it openly. He calls us to bring that particular person to the side, then bring two or three witnesses with you, then if they are still doing what they choose *then* do you bring it before the church(*if you have not done these things prior to an open rebuke then you are out of order*). Then the Bible says if they continue after that then cast them from the body as a heathen. This may sound harsh, but let me ask you a question. When an arm is infected so badly that it is in danger of infecting the whole body what do you do?

God is a God of order not disorder Satan loves to come at times such as this to cause division amongst the brethren, but where there is love there is unison and deliverance for the brethren and those who brought the rebuke?

Rebuttals. I speak as when you give the rebuke and to you who receiving the rebuke, you *will* get rebuttals from the crowd of those whom you are speaking to and those who have received a rebuke, rebuttal not! Because when this done it (*should most definitely be*)out of love and *not* hatred or bitterness. When God rebuked the disciples or anyone in the Bible it was only ever out of a place of Love. So, when you do these things it must *only ever be out of Love from the Lord Jesus Christ!* If you are feeling angry in the flesh it is best to keep your mouth shut, or you will be stepping before the Lord. *The steps of a good man are ordered by the Lord, and whatever a man planneth the will of the Lord always succeeds(Psalms 37:23, Proverbs 16:9).*

Also, as your brother I would not have you to be nonchalant to the fact that you will have those that will try to challenge you in your speech(*this is a part of the rebuttals*), so make sure that you are ready in the Holy Ghost that you may put Satan is his place and bring that fellowservant in the Lord or non-believer to more of the Truth in Christ

Jesus. God is a God of preparation so allow Him to prepare you in Word for such times for there will come a time in your life when you will have to defend the faith and you will have to open your mouth and speak. Will you cower in fear, or rise with authority and power in the Lord? And tell those devils about your God and put them in their places, while simultaneously showing love towards the person that you are speaking to(*at the same time pleasing the Lord!*). It's one thing to have power in the physical world, but when you have spiritual power it's a totally different battlefield and you *must* stay attentive my friends stepping where the Lord wants you to.

So fellow believers we have work to do in the Kingdom of God there are a lot of weeds, some body parts that need to be cut off, we are here to help the body correct? So help the body! We cannot worry about people's feelings! The Truth is the Truth and it doesn't matter who doesn't like it! Even if I get upset, who cares? We aren't go off of our feelings and God tells us that in His Word because our feelings don't outweigh God's wisdom, plus they are fleshly and not spiritual so move by the Holy Ghost no matter what people are saying either they will fall in line or they won't. Prophets where are you?! We need your prophetic voice! Don't remain quiet in this *season of the prophetic.* There are many *prophetic events* that are taking place at this very moment, *even as I am typing this to you.* As your brother and co-heir in Christ, I need you to open your mouth and let the God of heaven Who sits on High to speak through you to prophecy the unseen and to remind us of the things that we have forgotten! This is a spiritual outreach, the God in me is reaching out to you and I pray that by the Holy Ghost that you accept and grab ahold to the Lord's Mighty Hand that He may bring you forth into the field with me that we may work alongside together for the Lord of Glory that *He may be glorified!* Bless God for His outreaching and for His Glory that He has placed within us, *Christ our hope of Glory, Amen.*

Always be ye ready in the Lord for His coming, and for His call that when He calls you forth you will be also spiritually ready for the journey ahead of you. May God be glorified greatly in you prophets, may you bring forth the Glory of the Lord and bring once again bring the power of God into the churches that they may know and unlock the true power of God through your display of it and also by your words which are from the Lord, Amen and Amen. Selah. Praise God!

8. *The Times Are Upon Us: Cracking the Code for Spiritual Awareness of Time*

God has warned us countless time within His Gospel and Word of His coming and the events that happen in the perilous times. Many try to twist up the scriptures because of fear but the Lord has sent me to both clarify the truth and to denounce all the false claims of the end times. Like *when and where we shall depart, will be here during times of tribulation, when God will come.* All these answers are in the Word of God, but many try to denounce it because they want it to fit their philosophy therefore they begin claiming that they know when God is coming, *they even have a date!* Because of our sinful nature we think that we know all things and that all things must fit the way that we think, and that couldn't be further from the truth friends. Let go right into scripture and understand our destiny and when we shall go home!

One scripture that the King is pressing me to give right up from is Matthew 24:29, thus saith the Lord of Glory,

²⁹ *Immediately after the tribulation of those days shall the sun be darkened, and the moon shall not give her light, and the stars shall fall from heaven, and the powers of the heavens shall be shaken:*

³⁰ *And then shall appear the sign of the Son of man in heaven: and then shall all the tribes of the earth mourn, and they shall see the Son of man coming in the clouds of heaven with power and great glory.*

³¹ *And he shall send his angels with a great sound of a trumpet, and they shall gather together his elect from the four winds, from one end of heaven to the other.*

How is this misinterpreted? Right here does the Lord clarify His time of coming and *how* we will depart, where we will be. Let's break it down by the power of the Holy Ghost for this *is His Word*. God show us time *immediately after the tribulation of those days*, so we *will most definitely be in the days of tribulation friends, but then we are rescued by His shout to call us home, we are captured the angels and brought into glory with the King.* Again, *how is this misinterpreted?* Because just as I said you are fearful, because you have no real power and you cannot withstand this, so you have taught and deceive others(including yourself) to believing that you will not endure hardship for *the banner of Christ*, when the disciples did. God spoke to us when He was to come but just so that you try to deny it , it allows me to bring more clarification(*only by scripture of course*) more in depth the time of the second coming of the Lord Jesus Christ.

Jump to 2 Thessalonians 3:2-12, *¹Now we beseech you, brethren, by the coming of our Lord Jesus Christ, and by our gathering together unto him,*

² That ye be not soon shaken in mind, or be troubled, neither by spirit, nor by word, nor by letter as from us, as that the day of Christ is at hand.

³ Let no man deceive you by any means: for that day shall not come, except there come a falling away first, and that man of sin be revealed, the son of perdition;

4 Who opposeth and exalteth himself above all that is called God, or that is worshipped; so that he as God sitteth in the temple of God, shewing himself that he is God.

5 Remember ye not, that, when I was yet with you, I told you these things?

6 And now ye know what withholdeth that he might be revealed in his time.

7 For the mystery of iniquity doth already work: only he who now letteth will let, until he be taken out of the way.

8 And then shall that Wicked be revealed, whom the Lord shall consume with the spirit of his mouth, and shall destroy with the brightness of his coming:

9 Even him, whose coming is after the working of Satan with all power and signs and lying wonders,

10 And with all deceivableness of unrighteousness in them that perish; because they received not the love of the truth, that they might be saved.

11 And for this cause God shall send them strong delusion, that they should believe a lie:

12 That they all might be damned who believed not the truth, but had pleasure in unrighteousness.

Watch how the words of Christ, being the Word of God, align up with the words of the Lord with the words of Paul. Pay attention and read closely with an open mind, and harden not your hearts against my words for they aren't mine but the Lord's, Amen. In the very first scripture Paul speaks of the *gathering of the saints of God unto the Lord Jesus Christ,* and Christ stated and I quote, *" And he shall send his angels with a great sound of a trumpet, and they shall gather together his elect from the four winds, from one end of heaven to the other."* Then the timing is *also* the same, because God cannot deter from His Own Word, that in verse three and nine.

³ Let no man deceive you by any means: for that day shall not come, except there come a falling away first, and that man of sin be revealed, the son of perdition;

⁹ Even him, whose coming is after the working of Satan with all power and signs and lying wonders.

Look my friends with the eyes of the Spirit. God is said that He won't return until *after* tribulation correct?(*Go read Matthew 24:29-31 again.*) Then here in verse three and nine, "*..for that day shall not come..,*" then also *"Even him, whose coming is **after** the working of Satan with all power and signs and lying wonders."* There again we have the time, where we will be at the time of tribulation, and out departure confirmed by the Lord Himself which was enough in itself, but by His Grace again by Paul the apostle. We are to be gathered, the *saints of God only*, unto the Kingdom of heaven friends. Here can come the story of the ten virgins, because you believed the lie you have no more oil and therefore those who have the oil remaining only they were ready and could enter. When they went to the door and asked to come in the Lord said, *"Depart I know ye not."* And we see there even in teachings and parables that God *cannot* deter from His Word! And the reason I say that is because look *even closer* the Lord God did not come out again unto the last five virgins. Why? *Because He is only to return one last time friends!* Not two and three times, not in the middle of the tribulation, not before, but what do the scriptures say? "*Immediately after the tribulation of those days." Do ye see now how we will we here during persecution? Don't you understand that the Lord has to separate the wheat from the chaff? The goats from the sheep? The unfruitful branches on the tree? This is the dividing line on who is truly for God and who isn't!* And this is why many hate this philosophy(*which is the truth*) that we depart *after the days of tribulation! Because they know that if they are tested they will give in because they are afraid to lose their lives!(Your life was never yours to begin with. Did you ever give your life to Christ is you are holding on to it so tightly? When you know your destiny in Christ, and what He has done you no longer fear death because He doesn't and as* *having the Holy Spirit therefore we have the mind of Christ who was and is the Father.)*

You never really trusted the Lord you are just putting up a front, faking it until you make it. God sees your arrogance and pride in thinking that you will make it, and try to escape such persecution that is required to enter into glory. You will not escape no one will, not even me, and I am the one the Lord is using to write this. Like Jesus said, *"The servant is not greater than his lord. If they persecuted Me they will also persecute you."(John 15:20) So does this not tie a bow on things for you? Are you still in denial towards God's Holy Word and what it states?* I have a few more scriptures that the King of Glory is bringing to my attention that He would like me to bring before your eyes. God prophesied that this would happen not just to the disciples but to those that He hath chosen for His Glory, and all those who bear His Name(*John 13:18*). So my question to you my friends and fellowservants of the *Lord Jesus Christ* is, *Doth thou think thou art better than thy Lord?* Ask yourselves this question, are you unwilling to go through for the faith as God Himself did? He suffered persecution for the sake of His Own Name at the hands of men that *He created!* So why do you think that you wouldn't?

Jesus said in John 15:21, *But all these things will they do unto you for My Name's sake, because they know not Him that sent Me.* So to break it down to you, God being Jesus the Father He like I said could not deter from His Word because He is a God of Truth not lies, even *He* had to bow down and subject Himself to His Own Word that He may please the Father. And in this case the Servant, Who is Jesus, was not better than His Lord *which is the Father*! As the servant His too also had to suffer what the Father had spoke about, because He bore His Father's Name it was not His Own! *John 5:43, I am come in my Father's name, and ye receive me not: if another shall come in his own name, him ye will receive.* We see the power of God here, what is the Son's Name? It is, *Jesus the Christ*, but just so you know that Father and His Son are One Divine Being, they *even have the same Name! So if they are two different beings, how can they have the same Name?* It's not possible! Jesus was the God of the Old Testament as well as the New Testament, and with saying the He is a God of demonstration. He promised that the disciples and *all those who bare His Name* will go before kings, magistrates, and officials in the synagogues, we see that Christ did *just* as He the Father said we would go through as *His servants!* Our God is not Someone Who tells us to do something and He is not willing or hasn't done it Himself(*Our God is experienced in every area my friends*).

Before He spoke the words of the coming persecution He knew of Judas' decision in saying later before His own persecution, [16] *"And ye shall be betrayed both by parents, and brethren, and kinsfolks, and friends; and some of you shall they cause to be put to death.*

[17] *And ye shall be hated of all men for my name's sake."*

He knew of the coming betrayal from His Own brethren, but yet and still He did the will of the Father that He may be glorified! God doesn't want us to be without knowledge of such events, but many of you deny them each and every time they are brought up because you are afraid. Why? Because you have no true relationship Christ, therefore there is no power within you, making you constantly abounding in fear rather than the love of Christ Jesus. For God has not given us a spirit of fear, but of love, and of power, and a sound mind in having us to know the things that are ahead of us. I pray that you take these warnings that the King has brought forth already in His Word and through me at this very moment that this will not "take you by surprise" and because you see all these things happening around you, you take the bait that Satan hands out to save your own life. What is it to a man to gain the whole world yet lose his soul? Nothing. For Satan when he comes on earth as the Lord did to proclaim His Gospel, he promise you the world if you take his mark, and become a part of him or you will lose your life. Sadly many of you in the Church will bow down in fear and do it, betraying your Lord, brothers, sisters and for extra bonus give up your brothers and sisters to be killed to keep your life. I know this because Jesus warned me of it in His Word, those of you who are reading this get in your Word so that you can know these things which the Savior warns of(Luke 21:8-35, Mark 13, John 16, Matthew 24).

The denial of Peter was foreshadowing the events in the last days, for us toward another Peter denied ever knowing Christ, and His Person. Just like some of us will to one another when the time comes. Even though Jesus Christ was God, Peter wasn't denying God's power(blaspheming) but rather ever *being in fellowship with Jesus Christ* within His circle. And at that point Peter had not the Holy Ghost within him or his fate wouldn't have been what it came out to be, by denying Christ when the time comes that will follow blasphemy and what the enemy offers to you the ultimate betrayal against the Lord God. There is a slight difference He denied fellowship with Christ, but not blaspheme the power of God which is the Holy Ghost. Amen.

So we see here the persecution of the Lord Jesus unfolded and revealed, we think that Jesus was supposed to do that and we wouldn't have to endure the same. All of what He did was for His Name's sake and for us that we may overcome death just as He did in the same fashion my friends. *How can we overcome if we never even came?* Going forth into Jesus' prophecy over His Disciples and their persecution after His demonstration and resurrection from death. Let's go to the persecution of the disciples and followers of God in the book of Acts.

The Father promised persecution through His Son and demonstrated and His disciples followed knowing that it would happen because they all saw that the Lord hath done it, therefore they were prepared in mind and spirit(*For the Lord doth give us a sound mind to know the things which He speaketh and doeth, Amen. See 2 Timothy 1:7.*).

In Acts 4 Peter and John are captured by the priests, captains of the temple, and the Sadducees because they taught of the resurrection of Christ Jesus our Lord and how they had rejected Whom God has sent unto them. God said that they would go before rulers, kings, the priests and the scribes look at verses five through twelve. They testified of whose name they came in, the Lord's name, and what power they did it by. This was the first documented persecution of God's saints, they were warned by the high priests to no longer speak in the Lord's Name. What would you do after this? Would you be afraid to continue or will you continue with boldness in the Holy Ghost? This persecution that they faced was life threatening to the disciples, but instead of bowing down to the traditionalistic hypocritical high priests and Sadducees they recalled the words of the Lord that they would definitely be hated and threatened and brought before kings and rulers of the synagogues. Lo, the word of the Lord came to pass and it was powerful!

The disciples expected persecution going into their*(just like Jesus did going into His)*ministry it was not a foreign thing to them, it was not outlandish, they did not pity themselves like you do in saying, "Why should we have to go through these things? Our God is a loving God, therefore it isn't true!" You are in error! God's love is not contained by your thoughts or feelings! God's love goes *way* beyond any boundary *imaginable*, you could even say that it is a bit reckless. God's love goes deep to the core, His wants and desires are higher than ours. He wants to show us His undying love by showing us that even in these times that we will go through *He will comfort us*. God wants us to know how much we truly need and when we solely depend on Him in these times there will nothing stopping Him from protecting us as drastically as He did back in the day! We *shall be broken out of jails and the shackles of men, the earth shall open for us to swallow our enemies, grace shall reign over God's people in these last and evil days like never before! God's piercing Light will shine greatly in us and we shall shine like stars in this dark and perverse generation! This shall come to pass in Jesus Mighty Name, and I hope that those of you who read this are surely ready for these times. For they will either be a time of joy, or of great sorrow for you.*

Philippians 2:13- 15, [13] For it is God which worketh in you both to will and to do of His good pleasure. [14] Do all things without murmurings and disputings: [15] That ye may be blameless and harmless, the sons of God, without rebuke, in the midst of a crooked and perverse nation, among ye shine as lights in the world.

The disciples rejoiced after their persecutions because the Lord God had not only spoken these things but He was being glorified *in* these things, therefore *in* the disciples. God is worthy to be praised even in times of suffering and persecution because He spoketh of these things, and not only that but *even* ensured safety in the afterlife if we lost our lives in the process. Those of you who hate this doctrines are those who still fear death, but you say you serve God. Those who are of God are no longer of fear but are made perfect by His love, because fear is not of God but the opposite of Him because He is Love, Amen. We have a chance to be persecuted for a Holy Name friends, does that not bring joy to your spirit? A wretch like me gets to suffer at the hands of men for a Just and Holy King, and not only a King but the God of Heaven. We get to share in His sufferings, get a closer picture of what He went through to therefore *overcome with Him in sufferings.* Many of you have rejected what I have said even have skipped some of what I have written because it terrifies you, but take heed and rejoice for *the Father will have left us alone in that season and time(John 16:32)!* God knew going in that He would have to suffer, and while explaining this to His disciples we even see His sweet, undying love, teaching us as His sons how to go about *being sons of God* even in times of persecution knowing that He will not ever leave you lonely. Your "friends", colleagues, acquaintances, *even family members will leave you but the Father will never do so, for He hath made a promise to you and He will never break His promise spite of what we do against and to ourselves, He will never leave us comfortless. Praise God!*

⁴⁰ And to him they agreed: and when they had called the apostles, and beaten them, they commanded that they should not speak in the name of Jesus, and let them go.

⁴¹ And they departed from the presence of the council, rejoicing that they were counted worthy to suffer shame for his name.(Acts 5:40-41)

Understand this my friends that the disciples were so humble enough, and trusted God and allowed Him to be so control in their lives that they worried not about what men said but had authority from heaven to declare and to do exploits, *the acts of God before the eyes of men once again. God revealed to me the reason why Acts has its name, and how crucial this book is to us in these last and evil days!* Acts represents what acts God did through the hands of the apostles, then the crucial part of this book is both the Holy Ghost and the reasons for the faith! To ensure that we knew where the power came from and that is the Holy Ghost, and to know that we can receive this power if we *are surely* baptized in the name of His Holy Son, *Christ Jesus*, and have faith in the Father of heaven and earth. *This power* is so important for the times that are upon us my friends many of you are missing out of the power of God, and the sad thing is is that you won't even give what the Bible says about tongues a chance you deny it.

You will never truly unlock the Bible and its hidden messages that God with His Spirit will openly display before you if you allow Him. Many of you are only living for God on the surface, so therefore you will receive *surface knowledge about Him*. To the extent that you serve God and allow Him in, in the same fashion God will do the same. Not everyone can have His Spirit in them, but it is a sad thing that you want Him with you in you yet you deny Him at the same time. My spiritual heart aches for all of you whose mind is set on deny and denouncing the power of the Holy Ghost, and you wonder why you seem to be out of touch with God, or like you are not growing nor progressing because you have nothing inside you to want to go on. The Spirit of God is our Intercessor, our Energy and Stamina, our Determination when we don't feel determined, ye are still yet in the flesh! The flesh cannot please God, and the flesh that we are born into automatically rejects God they are enemies. So right now at this moment you are an enemy toward God because just like non-believers ye reject Him, disbelieve in Him, and ye also blaspheme Him by saying exactly what the Pharisees said(but I will put it in today's words so that you may understand) that the Holy Ghost, His Power(tongues) and the way He moves(causing us to jump, shout, and dance) is demonic!(If you are concerned whether or not you have committed this unpardonable sin, you have not done it. The Pharisees weren't concerned of this they only saw Jesus through their eyes of envy so ascribing the works of God, in *which He did*, made them feel better about themselves therefore they did so. Little did they realize they were cursing the Holy Ghost to His Face.) They blasphemed the Holy Ghost because they were trying to ascribing *the works of God* with Satan's demonic activity. How is it that jumping and dancing around at parties is not demonic, but at Church for God it is? Wouldn't you rather praise God rather than dance for the devil? Now, don't get it twisted, shouting is controlled by the Spirit of God(*God inhabits the praises of His people,*

He encourages it, or enables our praises to come through. He doesn't contain them like you are trying to do.).

And here is the scripture where the Pharisees did so in blaspheming the Holy One,

²⁴ But when the Pharisees heard it, they said, This fellow doth not cast out devils, but by Beelzebub the prince of the devils.

Like I said in the same way when you see someone dancing and jumping around for God you immediately ascribe it to the work of Satan. *Have you not read your Bibles?!* There is no way you could have if you are thinking this way! You want praise to be containable therefore traditional, so that you can have your way and so "things won't get too crazy". You want to just go to church with your hypocritical self, just sit in the pew listen to your pastor tell you about how much God loves you, but you're not even willing to show and tell Him how much you love Him in worship, praising and dancing. Listen, the more you stay stiff-necked like you are toward God everything else in your life with exude that in everything that you put your hands to. That job opening with slightly open, but never truly open for you(this represents your hearts toward God, never truly opening to Him nor His Power or His Word). I am coming the way I am by the Holy Ghost because you need to read/hear this and get out of that traditionalistic, stiff-necked mentality so that the promises of God can willingly flow within your lives that you may live *with God to the fullest here on this earth.* Also, you will *never* see the power of God for yourself as long as you deny His power. *How can you see something that you are always denying? Doesn't make sense does it?* That is the funny thing about it, people like that are the ones whose mouths are always going on complaining about how God isn't doing this and that when you are denying the power that God has *to do* what it is that ye are asking! You are denying what is *right in front of you my friends.*

I ask that you accept the Lord God *just as He is, accept His Love toward you and that as the Father of glory might show you His Power from on High like never before! He wants you, not your traditions and laws friends just your hearts that's all, I promise. Our God is not a God that requires anything but that because once He has captured your heart with His Love, He can show you His Love by the willingness to show His power toward you friends. Give God praise for His undying and never ending love that He shows through His Holy Son, Christ Jesus.*

Returning back to the *times*, and how we must prepare for such things there is no tribulation camp, but just as the Word Himself gave substance to His disciples when He was here on earth this *was their camp. Spending time with His servants, teaching them what they need to know, giving them wisdom on what to do and what not to do. God gave us tools friends, just as He gave His servants, the disciples, and He hands them down to us through His Word which is Him. Not only that but He gives us His Personal Spirit that we may fully comprehend His Glory, His Son, and of course His Word.* So to tie a bow on it spending time *with God* is the *only* way to truly *be ready* for these times my friends, there is no other *person* that you be spending time with more than Him, He is the One Who gives us substance that we eat, be full, and be prepared for our journey with Him in this season of persecution. Just the word alone brings fear, but didn't the Just One we served already conquer that over two millennia ago? Fear of death along with sin has already been done away with why are you still concerned about it? Be not afraid of such things for they have been placed by the Hand of God and His Power *under His feet*, and as I said before because *we serve Him they also have been placed under our feet.* Because we are with Him, He is with us, we are in Him, and He is in *us, the Holy Ghost of God we are His*. And the Lord Who reigneth over *all things* protects and guards the things He owns, and holds so dearly to His Heart.

I want you by the Spirit of God just to take in all that He has had me to say that you might move forward in the teaching of the Spirit. Understand this friends that the Father has promised a great victory and that is over death why do ye, I ask again, fear death? He has been conquered locked up, chained and wrestled down and defeated God has him under control now, He doesn't have any freedom to roam and take who he chooses. *Sin equals death, if ye are still in fear of sin ye still are living in it, yet you have an awareness of your sin. The worst feeling will be knowing all of these things and not applying them to you life while you are yet living on earth! God has given us choices and if we choose the one that leads us to destruction He will be the one to guide you to the place in which you worked towards.* I am going to say this in defense of the faith and my God, *God giveth and He taketh away blessed be the name of the Lord,* and also people going to hell and *their decision* to go there has absolutely *nothing* to do with the Lord. You are set with a set of decisions and whether you think so or not you will choose one and you will reap the benefits of that decision. Many of you non-believers especially atheists think that God is forcing you to believe in Him, that if you don't hell is your home. My God is not forceful, *like I said you have a decision to make! He leaves it up to you whether or not your will follow His Way or not.* What is *preposterous* I'd say is that you think that you can enter a place where the Man that created it you don't believe in. That's nonsense! Because by believing *in the place called heaven* and *in God is the ONLY Way to heaven, there is no other way guys that simple. And that the only way is through His Son, Christ Jesus, Whom He, the Father is. Because when you accept God you accept everything that comes with Him. Heaven is not yours to claim without Him, because He created and it is His. It is His to share, not yours to try and grab a hold of like a thief without permission.*

You may not like this truth, but the Lord God of heaven sent me to speak these words unto you that you may know the truth in full, whether you accept it or not has nothing to do with God or me, but it's up to you friends! Those of you who are non-believers that are reading this book you have the choice to make, the ball is in *your* court, but your problem is is that you don't want to have to face the consequences for what you choose, you want to have someone to blame and that is *my God. You may not want to follow His Way and that is fine, but don't blame Him for the decision that you know brings you to hell. He has nothing to do with your decision that is why He gave free will to us men that we may have the right to choose! He will have nothing to do with your decision so keep Him out of your pool of blame! If God was to blame He wouldn't be God now would He? He would be like us, a common man, but He isn't! He is the High and Just King Who rules with the Staff of Righteousness Whose Judgements are fair and pleasing. Praise God.*

God gives a clear description of the perilous times through His servant, Paul, describing the attributes of men. As in being trucebreakers, evildoers, etc. Allow me to ask you all one question, *How is everything that Bible states about the perilous times here and you deny it?* You try to make things make sense to yourselves according to the philosophy that you created *not God.* You try to make it make sense that you shouldn't be here when things take this turn, but yet you are a part of the very things that He describes. No? God warns of synagogue (church) of Satan, who once were of the truth but fell due to sin and the denial of God and His Power and the Deity of His Son. This my friends is called the Apostate Church, God tells us and warns us of the evil that it will entail. They forget the teachings of Christ and His Deity, openly will deny Him as God, and not respect *Him as God. When Christ is the one Whom we are born into through the Spirit of the Father in which He is!* This Church will began to receive all doctrines except the one that holds the truth, then they shall be utterly destroyed by the Political Babylon in which Satan will take over and rule. For my Father has warned of such things, yet you cannot see it because you have blinded yourself with your own darkness and are unwilling to come to the truth of God in Christ Jesus. God's anger is against you ministers who know the ways and teachings of His Son, yet you lead the flock astray to a place of condemnation in which you will be if you do not return to the Lord thy God.

I love you all, may the Holy Ghost be glorified in you, and may you serve with all your heart, soul, and mind, Amen. Bless God the Father and the Lamb of God Who sits on the Right Hand of the Living and Just God. Amen!

9. *Worries, Doubts, and Concerns*

With all of this knowledge and revelation it can be both invigorating and almost scary. Don't, however, think in your flesh because you must remember that this work we are doing is not by our hands but the hands of the Spirit of the Lord. The work that we do for God *is Spirit*, so we must *let the Spirit of God* handle it friends. All that is required of us is faith, but not faith alone and the "work" applied to that is done by the invigoration of the Spirit, put faith towards what you want to plant in the field and the Gardener with tell you what you must do to plant it.

Let the Almighty King rule over you with His Power for great things happen when you do. Trust me the King will not leave you in lack, especially because you are His child, and He is your Father.

Every person that comes to the faith, and is even deeper in the faith have second thoughts about what God called them to do, even when it comes to just believing *in God*. I, too, have had these thoughts but them the King would remind me of all that He has done for me, and *how could He not be real?* The event of me receiving His Ghost could not have been faked!

And by this event happen(outside of my control) and by that happening according to the Word of God signifies to me that this Deity *is real*. The fact that God said that He was the *only* God, and He answered in the way that He did signifies to me that He is My God, and He is the *only* God that exists. No other God answered me in my time of trouble, "Jesus!" I called and He said, "Yes, My son." Now, if we are thinking logically if this was Muhammad, Buddha, or Allah they would have corrected me in my called to them. No other god answered me, *none else.*

No God would ever allow themselves to be called by a god that doesn't exist. The people who serve, Allah, believe that he is the only god, the true god. But he didn't answer me. I reached down deep to really search Who God was and when I called on the *name of God, that is Jesus Christ, He answered me.* You may get angry, but I am coming from a place of total truth, and boldly that Jesus is the only God that exists and that has *ever* existed. This is not competition, it *just is*. My *Jesus* has answered me with His voice and by His own authority, and because He is a Spirit or *the Spirit of God* He speaks to *my spirit.*

I noticed that when Jesus is spoken about automatically there is a negative thought or connotation, why is that? He is all good, all loving, all graceful, all patient, all forgiving and yet His Name is still blasphemed on public television(He is everything that the world needs right now in this hour! True love, peace, and joy it's all in Jesus Christ!). It is because demons are in the system and try to block or silence the name of Jesus or any discussion of Him quickly because they know that there is power in His Name. Notice in the speech of Chris Pratt, he mentioned the name of the Lord Jesus Christ but it was cut out of it. Why? Because demons know their authority and wish not to deal with Him so that they can have their way with sin and evil. You, reading this may be apart of this censorship, why have they told you to do this only to the Christians, and to Jesus Christ and not the other gods such as Allah, Buddha, etc? There is truth in Jesus Christ and they know it, this isn't speculation or conspiracy theories but fact and truth. Don't believe me?

Look at how in almost every movie and t.v. show they are willingly slandering the name of Jesus like it is just another name. And that is the devil's goal to *make it just another name.* To denote and pull down the name of God from being the Highest of High. So with saying that, this should encourage you to see that God is real, and by limiting His Name in speeches and other important media there is more to it than what it seems.

As I was typing the LORD was showing me that these demons that have been sent out are demons sent to uproot and destroy, and wherever the name of Jesus Christ is dominant or powerful they are to find some way to stop it from flowing in that place to contain souls from being freed from the power of sin. These are evil and vile creatures keep yourselves holy before the Lord that you might spot them off from afar that they may not gain traction where you are. "Remain in Jesus Christ for He has our salvation and in Whom we trust, and will deliver us into our true home in heaven," saith the Lord Jesus Christ. Understand this my friends we are in a spiritual battle for souls, allow our God to move freely within you so that as He is lifted high men are being drawn unto Him for salvation.

Be ye not concerned about demons, witches, and their spells our power was given from heaven therefore we triumph over them with the power of God, the Holy Ghost. The witches know about the Holy Ghost and they too fall in line when the authority figure steps in. Jesus the head of all principality shows Himself strong in *His Spirit, but* we must have His Spirit within ours(we must become one with Him and His Son) in order for this to happen. Just as I said before these demons will pounce onto you just as others did those exorcists who tried casting out demons. (Think not this will not happen to you, you have been warned.)

I praise God through His Son, Jesus the Mighty Christ, for being so strong and trustworthy in my walk with Him. All my doubts, worries, and concerns disappear when He comes to mind for He was and is more than a man but He is my Father and the Gracious Hand toward me in my struggles. He has carried me through tests and trails that I may see His Power firsthand that I might declare Him and His Son to you (for they *are one).*

Jesus cleared up doubt before the eyes of the disciples and He saith, "Blessed is he that see the Me not, and believes in Me." So in this material and carnal world by you trying to perceive the things in the

Spirit, you must have the *eyes of the Spirit* in order to do so. Don't be like the doubting Thomas and only would have to see to believe! Faith cometh by *hearing the Word of God.* So listen to God and believe in His Word trust and know that He has it all planned and mapped out for His child. You are the son/daughter *He is the Father let Him work!*

One thing that you need to learn from this chapter that as a believer we are self-sufficient in Christ's sufficiency, that God is our Power, Strength, Guide, Perfecter of our Faith and He is the Righteous One and He will take us into glory. Nothing and no one can help us but God, yes, He will use others to help us but ultimately keep your eyes focused on the King of Glory. The world hates our standards and our way of living, and they will try to get you to compromise your faith in accepting certain laws that are passed forgetting the Word of God and what He states. They will say, "Doesn't God tell you not to judge? Didn't He tell you love and not hate? Didn't Jesus sit with sinners?" Don't allow Satan to bait you with his deceitful words, his children will speak and do what he says. God was not a friend to the sinners, and was He equally yoked to those that did evil deeds, but He was a Minister(Matthew 9:12) and a Teacher of the Gospel of God to the people. The thing about Jesus is that He stood out among the non-believers and the Church, because He was truly sold out to God. The problem with the Church of today is that we have forgotten who we are and why we are sent! We go forth ready to preach the gospel, but because you are not truly sold out to God, your flesh takes you over with the diverous lust that you supposedly allowed God to deliver you from(Matthew 13:1-9, 18-21).

"Come out from them," **says the Lord Jesus,** *"And be ye separate, that I may know My children from the children of Satan, that I may know My holy flock from the wicked one. For I AM a Shepherd of all things good, therefore if you are a part of what is evil you have taken up arms with the evil one and have partnered with him to destroy Me and My people and what we stand for, and that is holiness,"* **saith the Lord, the Great Shepherd of God's people!**

You become an enemy of the faith and toward God when you began to handle and taken partnership with the enemy and those that handle(touch, deal with or in) darkness. There must be something that divides us from the world if there is no difference there is no way to salvation. Why do you say that Brother Jordan? Because where there is no faith there is no access, and where there is not Word of God in a person there is not a place for God to flow. God does not deal with corruption nor does He deal in mixture. All of this acceptance of false doctrines and faiths to create "peace" is only destroying you and the others that take part in this blasphemy. God is not pleased Church, what and Who gave you your beauty and glory was Jesus Christ your Father and Husbandman. He clothed you when you had no clothes, he loved you when the world cast you out. Yet you continually turn to Barabbas, the murderer, for love but he is not capable of loving you the way that your God the Lord can!

The flesh, the carnality the evil thing that we spoke of before has found its way back into the Church into the hearts of God's people! We were once saved and filled with the Holy Ghost, but now we are filled with something else that isn't God. You go to the strip club as a pastor, because your wife is not doing the things that you would like her to do because she is a woman of holiness. As a wife, the pleasure that you seek in your husband you find in other men(deacons) in the Church. I am not here to bash nor to hate, but to love the(literal) hell(and all that it consists of) out of you. Don't get me wrong, you are accountable for what you do, but as a minister of the faith my job is to ensure that my fellow co-heirs in Christ are *holding themselves accountable*, keep them in line with the Word of God using *righteous judgements* by His Word to ensure that you are following Him.

Love the Lord your God with your whole heart, seek Him while He may be found, because there will come a time where God's Light and His people will be a hidden treasure that will be hard to find. We will arise occasionally, we will have seemed to had been snuffed out but we will be underground, or in a place not known to man. We will be among you, but not among you. You will hear us, but not see us for word will have been passed to you about the works of God that were made manifest in us. You will seek comfort but not find it, even death but it will be hidden from you. The same people you wish to kicked off the face of the Earth will be the same people that you will desire to stand by in the end but you will have chosen a side and it won't be the one that you thought would save your life. A great sting will hit the land after choosing this, and God will be known again as King and even your ruler at the time will acknowledge that God was the One that hath done this because God is his enemy and God triumphs over him. You will know who this man is *after* he has so easily deceived you, and it will be a terrifying discovery but you will be trapped with no savior because you will be the one that had condemned yourself with *your choice and freewill.*

Fear not, for this is only a warning to you that you might began living again accordingly to the Word of God and to the statutes of the Great King! Never doubt, never be concerned nor worry about a thing for with God all things are possible, and that is why we follow and *love Him with our whole heart our place in heaven is secure. Amen, thank You Jesus!!!*

10. Jesus Christ is the Living Water, our Holy One

In the last day, that great day of the feast, Jesus stood and cried, saying, " If any man thirst, let him come unto Me, and drink. He that believeth on Me, as the scripture hath said, out of his belly shall flow rivers of living water." (But this spake He of the Spirit, which they that believe on Him should receive: for the Holy Ghost was not yet given; because that JESUS was not yet glorified.) John 7:37-39.

God is good, and great He is all the time to all people, to all the creatures of land, to all the nations. The fact that Christ was to be glorified for the Holy Ghost to come is very significant to our legacy as Christians and the Father's temple and household of faith. His Name was glorified, His soul(Spirit) was glorified, and His Person as God was glorified. Because as Jesus was Glorified so was the Father in heaven because (hopefully you have come to the conclusion by now that) God is *One God and One Lord Who rules and reigneth over all living things above, all things below the earth and the things in the earth.*

Because Christ is the Rock, the literal image and all God in One, whatever comes from Him is of water that is increasingly and perpetually flowing. For whoever believes on Him shall receive the Holy Ghost in which we know is the Spirit of God, which teacheth(1 Corinthians 2:9-16) and helps us to know Who the Father is with the Son. For it is the Holy Ghost's job to reveal both the Father and the Son(that's why it's important to seek the Holy Ghost because without Him we have neither the Father nor the Son, because only *they* can reveal *Him*.)

When God comes *forth*, He comes with *full power* and *is fully Himself*. Tell me should we worship a pillar of clouds because it was used as a symbol of God? Should we worship *the mountain* that God stood upon to speak to Moses and the children of Israel? *God forbid!* No, we should worship the One Who is speaking! What I mean by these questions is that God can come in any form, but that does not mean that He is not fully God, nor should we worship the matter that He comes in but *Him and Him only*. Let me put it this way if I wear a costume, am I not still fully Jordan? Just because God humbles Himself and comes in the form of servant to serve, and made in the likeness of men doesn't mean that He is not God(Ephesians 2:6-8).

Jesus Christ is the Living Water, and He is our Rock and our Holy One. He is the same Rock that quenched the thirst of the people of God, the children of Israel. Once He was pierced, beaten and His blood began to flow He was the physical Rock that flowed to bring salvation to the souls of those He loved, which is the whole world. God be praised for His Ultimate Sacrifice upon the tree! once He was struck, then that opened up the ability for us to drink from His soul(Spirit) that we may have our thirst quenched by receiving the Holy Ghost of God. Once God's Soul was in ours we would then be satisfied, by having Christ's holy presence surrounding us and *within us*. Jesus kept Himself, humbled himself, remained out of the "in-crowd" that He may keep Himself holy for us that when He would give His sacrifice to Himself, it would be perfect and well-pleasing to God the Father, which is the Lord of glory(1 Corinthians 2:6-8)that was crucified.

We see God's Character in abundance, willing to share His body, be a piece of our Sacrifice by saying, *"Eat of my flesh and drink of My blood."* Also, that *He is the bread of Life, that we should eat of to live.* That once we taste and see the *goodness of God*, them and only that can we began really consume the Word of God as needed because we have *sampled Him.* Those of you who are deep in the Gospel and have been in ministry for thirty plus years, you should be on meat now, no longer on milk. All the things that I have spoken of ye shall have already known. God is a Teacher and He is *He that teacheth, the Holy Ghost, that we may know the deep things of God.* Do you have His Spirit, or do you deny the power thereof after all these years? Is your garment portraying godliness? Is not your bowels which is on the inside covered with gold and bronze because of the knowledge of God, and the fear of God? Some of you think that because you have been in ministry for years and years you have a say so and what goes, and you only. But I would admonish you to remember the Lord thy God and His statutes that He is the One with the last say so, and the *only say so when it comes to the Kingdom of God, because He is God not you.* You have pushed those who wish to learn the Gospel for the salvation of their souls outside onto the street, you have not shown them the love of God just as Jesus our LORD and Savior hath done. Are ye followers of God, or followers of each other? Ye glorify one another before you will glorify God, you acknowledge the pastors and bishops before God is acknowledged. You break a sweat to ensure that the master bishop is pleased with you, but forsakes the council of God.

I come to you in love that ye would not forsake and continue to forsake your God that He might rule in your hearts as the God of peace that He is. That you may be holy and perfect just as He is holy and perfect our Father, Jesus Christ. I am not a perfect Christian, but I am not of what I speak of or the Lord would not be using me to bring this forward to rebuke you of your wrong. I rebuke the enemy and the seed that you have allowed him to place in your hearts, and I say that you come back to the fold and the body of Christ that you acknowledge God, the Christ as the Living Godhead of His body, that you would remove yourselves from the altars and high places that you have built with your hands for one another. As I have warned you before if you do not step down God will use His mighty Hand to knock down pedestals that ye sit upon. Tell me, have ye read of the Pharisees? They were the ones that gave Jesus a hard time because of Who He was and their denial of God's power in Him. Because they forsook God, they recognized Him not when He came. But jealousy, rage, and wickedness was put against the Lord of glory because He could and wouldn't fail and fall into the traps that they had set for Him(Romans 1:21-23). Tell me, why are you like these men for the past? Ye have linked up with the spirit of pharisaism, rather that the Spirit of the Lord, and whoever comes with authority not given from you and know not whence they came you try to tear them down! Is this the way of God? I can simply say no. And I know and perceive in the Spirit of the Living God that ye do not like me for my words in which I speak, but I say unto you that the words I speak in this book are not mine but of the Father and the Son's Who is He the One and True God whose power in the Holy Ghost in Whom He dwells and is. These are God's words. I pray that you would come to where God is that He may draw Himself toward you that you might know the deep and heavenly things of Spirit of Jesus the Living Christ and God.

Eat of the flesh and drink of the blood of Christ your Savior that you may know Him as He is. *The Bread of Life, the Living Water, the Head Cornerstone, the Savior and Christ of the whole world.* I ask that ye would trust in Him with your whole heart today that He may do His works in you. God calls out through me to you that you may not be destroyed and die in your sins. It is a dangerous to know the things of God and not do them, even more dangerous fall into the hands of the living *God(Hebrews 10:31).*

Also, that you may not be confused to eat and to drink of the meat and blood of Jesus is to consume Him spiritually by reading His Word and to drink of Him by His Spirit, for He is our substance that benefits us both physically and spiritually. All things proceed forth from Jesus, the Most High, that because all power was given to Him of both heaven and Earth, He was equal to God(Ephesians 2:6-7). *"God hath made that same Jesus, Whom you have crucified, both Lord and Christ." (Acts 2:36)* So God literally exalted, Jesus, as God, for He was both God and man at the same time! Glory to God the Most High God and Father, Whose Name alone is powerful enough to cast out demons and to heal and to set free those in bondage!

All the knowledge of the Spirit of God, and His mindset dwells in Christ for our brother, Paul, is he that saith to the Lord of hosts, "Let this *mind* be in You, which was also in Your Son, Christ Jesus." (*Ephesians 2:5)* So, our brother Paul recognized the Oneness of God in Jesus Christ, that, yes, Jesus was the Godhead bodily. All the attributes and who God really was was in Christ Jesus, He made all things known about His Father *as the Father incarnated as the Son of God! Praise the Living God of Creation!* So when we have Father we also have the Son, when we have the Son you also have the Father, and he that hath both of them together *in* them equally have the Holy Ghost, who is the Spirit of the Living God. So Paul was simply implying that God's mind be in His, and how can this be so if a man hath not the Spirit of God dwelling in him? Not so, God has declared that He is One countless times, God doesn't need a counsel, for He a Wise Counselor among Himself alone, "There is no other god" the Lord said, "I know not any."(Isaiah 44:8). *The One True God was revealed to us by God(Romans 1:19-20).*

Tell me, why would God give such Glory and Honor to such a man? To someone else, even? God doesn't share His glory with anyone else *because* it would take the focus off of Him! Anything that was in the way of His people focusing on Him He removed *because* He was all they needed! Gods they built with their hands, statues that can not breathe nor see even though they are molded with eyes. Nor, can they hear even though they are molded with ears, but because God cannot be handled by men, and is *above* that makes Him outside of things therefore *God.*

"*I AM THAT I AM, heareth him that I sent to speak to you, I have given him words to speak that no man can find on their own. I have given him insight on Me and My kingdom and all mysteries concerning thereof. I AM God, and I speaketh with thee, hear Me as you read the words that I hath given My son and servant. He comes not by his own power but by Mine, heareth him and look upon the demonstration and fruit that I bring thereof through him,*" *saith the Lord of hosts.* **Thank You Jesus!**

My God, my God is all powerful and Wonderful, never seeks men's counsel in whom He chooses for if so I would not be in this position! But because God loves me, and looks past all my mistakes and evil I have done in my past. I come not of my own power, but by God's as He had said in the previous passage. You may not be familiar if you are a new believers how God speaks to His people, sometimes He will give words to write down then speak, or speak right when He says to without writing it down. Those who know God and follow His Spirit will know in the Spirit that the words in which I speak are from His mouth not my own friends. God be praised!

So with saying that, Jesus should be exalted above all men, all living things because He is our Holy One, the Creator of this world, the Living Water in which we go to when we thirst, our Love and Savior. He is all these things, so just as *even God* acknowledged Him as both Lord(Supreme Ruler) and Christ(The Anointed, Holy One of God) so should we. Since we follow God, we should follow Him in Christ and in Christ only do we follow Him for *they are one.* Why do you think that the whole world mocks and scourns the name of Jesus, on national TV and media so that His Name cannot be seen as strong and saving?

Because it is the name of God! Because thou not knoweth who you serve, you know not that the name of God is being blasphemed before you.

I ask that you see and understand Jesus, that because we have Him we have all things. *He that spared not His own Son, but delivered Him up for us all, how shall He not WITH HIM also freely give us all things? (Romans 8:32.)* Because when God gave us Jesus, He was giving us *all things! Amen!* Those of you that know the doctrine of Christ, yet teach another doctrine(willingly to demean Christ and His doctrine) if you are reading this and understand that you are in the wrong this is your opportunity to come from those false doctrines created by devils to destroy you! If you do not come out but continue ye are condemning yourselves to fire and brimstone because you have not the Savior that you speak of nor His Father.

All things were given unto Jesus, and in Him we have life, we have our joy, we have our strength to fight the good fight and be mighty soldiers for Him. Be not afraid as evil increases and the world struggles to put a halt on our doctrine and way of living. Remember what the King of heaven hath spoken, He Who created *all things in existence* that, *"..Upon this rock I will build My Church; and the gates of hell shall not prevail against it."* No matter what it may look like in this world, no matter how dark this world seems to get know that our God has us and He is *still the Light that shineth in the darkness! And nothing can put out the Light of God!*

We are His saints, His people so we must remain faithful to Him as He is to us. We must not allowing vain deceits, those who speak false doctrines to corrupt us, but we must bury the doctrine of Jesus Christ in our hearts that we might know what to say, and when to say it, to use our wisdom and knowledge that He hath given us for such a time as this. Nothing can stop us when we have faith in the King of kings and the Lord of lords because that gives Him access to work in us and through us. For we shall do mighty exploits for His Namesake and we shall glorify Him with our bodies. Think not that the enemy has won just because be slays us with the sword, know the even in the physical death God is glorified. Satan thinks that he has won, but he is just pushing us closer to God. And just when he thinks he's rid the earth of God's people and Light that when God will come and He will intervene in Satan's ruling and God will destroy him! And things will be set back into order just as God saw it before the foundation of the earth. Us with Him, Him with His people us singing, "Howdy! Howdy!" Unto the Lord God Almighty forever worshipping Him and praising Him for eternity give Him what He deserves. We will finally be able to freely worship and go higher than we have ever gone before! Are you excited? Are you pumped for the return of Christ? I am, I can't wait to see Him on His throne in *all* His glory, for Him to be fully known by me even as I am fully known. We go from glory to glory, as in a mirror, but one day will see the face of God as looking in the mirror, clearly see Him!

My heart yearns for the goodness of God, my soul pants like a deer for water for God. If I didn't have God it would be like I am malnourished from not drinking water, I would eventually get over dehydrated and die. This is how my soul is for God! Have you found all your necessities in men and materials things? Have ye forgotten the God of heaven and how He has blessed you with those things? Have you left Him behind? Forget not that He is the Source, not the resource, all things flow from God, Jesus Christ our Living well of water. How can you get so caught up in the things of this world that things that *God* gives and not Him?

Some of us have gotten caught up with our blessings and not the Giver of those blessings, and you wonder why you can't be blessed with the next thing! Because ye have taken our God for granted, ye want not Him but what He can give. To help keep yourselves in need of God, tell the Lord, "If You are not in this blessing God, I don't want it." This will be hard for some of you, because you wish not to serve God but to get all the benefits thereof. But I say unto you that God sees your heart and His face is turned against you, because ye wish to use the treasures of God for the things that are of corruption and *not of God. God spoke to me* concerning the hearts and the intents of men, that they are using His Name as a stepping stone for their *own* personal glory. That when it comes for God to get the glory in a situation they'll give it to themselves for personal gain and the Spirit's glorification for His Grace and Love. Let's look in scripture to compare similarities between today's world and then.

Flip to Acts 12:21-23, *21 And upon a set day Herod, arrayed in Royal apparel, sat upon his throne, and made an oration unto them. 22 And the people gave a shout, saying, It is the voice of a god, and not of a man. 23 Immediately the angel of the Lord smote him, because he gave not God the glory: and he was eaten of worms, and gave up the ghost.*

God said, " My glory will I not give to another, neither My praise to graven images." (Isaiah 42:8) Herod was haughty in his apparel and speech lifting himself up as God with the glory that should have gone to God, but God quickly knocked him down where he stood through the angel. God warned me that if I continued in my evil everything that I touched would be as ash when someone blew upon it, everything would fall apart if I did not respect Him as My God. So I say unto you, whatever evil that you have connected yourself with as a man or woman of God *disconnect yourself with the quickness! For God is building a home and temple that He may dwell in, and you are either in or out no in between it's time to make a choice! Jesus prepare a way before us Your people that we might follow and not depart, let Your commandments keep us steady upon the road of salvation, keeping us until we reach You, O God in heaven!*

Jesus came by His Own power to declare the power of God that men might know that it's possible to inherit this power through the sonship of Christ Jesus. Not until Christ came could we have the mind of sons and daughters of God, and have that mind to be children of God. Because remember the power that was given to Christ Jesus, John 1:12-13,

12 But as many as received Him, to them He gave power to become the sons of God, even to them that believe on His Name: 13 Which were born not of blood, not of the will of the flesh, nor of the will of man, but of God.

(Because as we recognize the name of God, we recognize the name of the Father as His sons, then we become sons of God.) Read with interpretation from the Spirit and you will never fail in understanding Him. Once you realize who Jesus is you realize who you are, because came to declare the identity of the Father and Who He was. In doing so, He revealed all the things that were shut up about God, that He was *like* a physical Person that you could speak to; has ears, eyes, a mouth to

speak, a body, that He is a Spirit that the physical manifestation of God's glory could only come through One Man, and that is God. Amen. I pray that ye do not harden your hearts against this doctrine for the doctrine that I speak is that same of what Christ preached: His equality with His Father and that *there is and always was One God, One Lord, and One Savior, ever!* And His Name was Jesus Christ, the Holy One of God(Isaiah 43:15), God Incarnate, also called *"the glory of the LORD,"* or *"the manifestation of the LORD".*

What God wants is for us to understand Him in all fullness of His Power and Deity, to be free in the knowledge by Him; of there being *One God.* He wants a personal relationship with you, by you having His Spirit *in* you that He might flow freely within in you and through you that His power will be made manifest in you. There are only a few of us who know the truth *and live in*, or how the Word of God put it, "Blessed is he that are hearers and doers of the word of God(*Luke 11:28*)." There are those who hear the word of God, rejoice even but when tribulation comes for the Word you cower in fear, you are afraid of the benefits of the Gospel of God. Be not afraid of what men can do to the body, but of the One Who can destroy the body and soul in hell. We are meant to suffer, because through persecution do I understand what my Lord went through, and not only that I become a partaker in the sufferings of Christ therefore giving my life to Jesus fully.

Understand this, that our God moves in ways that we may not understand but He is always in control He never sleeps nor slumbers because He has no need to do so. He is always alert and eager to make sure that all things are set the way should be for His Children. Coming to the knowledge of such persecution for living holy unto God, at first seemed scary, even illogical that if God loved me why should I endure such things? A question that arises from the fruit of my lips now is, "God loved His *only* Son but He caused Him to go through and suffer for His people, so why shouldn't I for *Him*?" Also, too, "I confess that I am willing to die for my friends, but why not for God?" Nothing that can be said will ever change my mind as to what we will endure, I would be afraid and cowering away if my Savior, Jesus Christ, wouldn't be there with me as He was with His Son. For He had said before His time of persecution, " You will all leave me alone, but I will not be alone, for my Father is with Me."(John 16:32)

Is it shameful to die for God, is it something to be afraid of? It should. Our nature is based off rejecting God, His Goodness, Truth, and Righteousness because we were born into the nature of sin and evil therefore making our intentions and ways *evil before the Lord.* Only our desires in this state of mind matter, nothing else; we are selfish making ourselves number one and the center of everything. Dying for righteousness to the carnal man in foolishness and nonsense, never will he truly understand like a man of the Most High would. And again if you are a newcomer to Christ, *you will think, "If your God loves you why would He want you to endure such things?"* And I will make a rebuttal to that question with a set of questions, *"Why would you die for your family members? Why would you die for your friends? Why would you promise to get beat up for them if it came to it? If they loved you why should you go through those things for them?"* It's because it deals in righteousness you understanding is not there, only the Holy Ghost can give such teaching that you may understand, that is what He is having me to do here and now. See this, Christ Jesus our God and Only Mediator saw fit that He His sacrifice would be perfect and just right that you might live. He put Himself last, because all He saw was you, that He would have a chance to be *closer* to you. That even in persecution, you would know that your King went through the same thing and that He is there with you just like He was there for His Son, and He was God the Son! Jesus was enough in Himself (because He was the Father) so in conclusion Jesus, the Father, is all you need to do the work that He calls for us to do, Amen.

I bless you, O Father, O Heavenly and Holy One. You have created me for such purposes that I might be Your servant and your minister in the land that the people of God and those who are lost to know about the True God, and that is You, O Mighty Jesus, my God. Your Name is strong enough to fight for us, in these times of persecution Your Light will shine for we will be persecuted for righteousness just as it states in Your Holy Word and we shall rejoice with song and dance because in this You, O God will be glorified and Your Majesty of your

Kingdom and Your Son will be shown even in death(the physical), and we shall ascend into Your Arms that are stretched out wide that You might receive us unto Yourself, that we shall live forever with You, O God of Zion and Heaven, Amen!

In conclusion of this chapter: Know this my friends that the Lord of hosts, loves your with all of His heart, all of mind, and all of His soul. Anything that you could possibly need it can be found alone in, Christ Jesus, Who is God and always was since the beginning. I was chosen by Him to declare Him and His Son that you might know their equality in each other and that They are indeed One God, that the Living Water that you seek for your souls is Jesus the Living Christ our God. I am one of many that will declare such things is a profound way! Many prophets will arise, many teachers, many pastors, many apostles, and many evangelists will arise to declare the Gospel of Christ and use the power of God, which is the Holy Ghost to truly demonstrate the power that Jesus shewed when He was upon the earth in His Ministry. I declare now in the name of Jesus that as you read this those of you who have heard the Spirit of God speaking through my words, that your spirits are rising to the occasion for Christ that you might get to work just as the disciples of Jesus in the old day did. You are already followers of Jesus Christ, this is a call-to-action, jump aboard! Much love to you, and may you be mighty in Christ Jesus our Lord, Savior and God, Amen.

11. I, the Father, speaketh

Your Father in heaven speaks this to you, I am but a messenger of His. His Words will penetrate the stones of your heart and turn it to flesh. Those that have ears hear what the Spirit speaketh, " *I AM the One Who declared the Father of heaven in the earth, I AM also He that speaketh when my Name is called upon, I AM He who is also called the Holy Ghost. I AM the Father that created all of His children, all colors, shapes and sizes, I created all of you. None of you go out of My sight where I cannot see you. I know your whereabouts, your current situations, all things concerning you. I AM building and establishing a Church in which I AM the Head thereof, not the pastors, not the bishops, not the teachers, nor the prophets, but Me only, your King of Glory, and He that is called your God. My Spirit is to be poured out upon all living things that all of you might understand Me, and might know Me as I AM to be fully known by you. I brought forth this man, Jordan Irving, to be a spokesperson, one of many to declare the equality of My Son and I, to help men to understand My nature and how you should live under the King of Israel, the God of Holiness and Creation. He is not powerful on his own, but all of what he teaches he has heard from Me, the Holy One, and those who know Me with hear his word for they are Mine, not his. Many of you will try to stop him, but he will be as a dam that is impossible to patch up, and the water that floweth down from him will scatter you here and there. For the power that is in him has been imparted by Me, the Holy Ghost, and no one can stop Me, therefore because He serves Me, and because of his faith he cannot be stopped. For he is Mine, and I AM his, and no one can separate him from Me, for I have captured him in his time of despair and brought him to heavenly places in Christ Jesus, My Son and I. I, too, will impart power to those who seek Me, but to those who want this power for their personal gain, I will expose for all to see. You will be as a thief that has been caught, and I will be the judge to issue the sentence to you. And my angels will put you in your rightful place. Everything that I have spoken thus far shall commence soon after My son, Jordan, has begun and ye shall know then that I have truly chosen him. Validation comes not from men and their value of validation, but it only comes from the One with a righteous eye. And I have seen him and have known him, his heart wants nothing but to bring glory to My Name. You will have your speculations of him, in the way that he moves for it will be nothing that you have ever seen in this day and age, but you will remember these very words and then I will reveal to you the work that I hath called you to do. You will no longer be offended of him, for you will remember these words and will tell others of the words of the Lord. He is sent to declare, to roar the gospel of God, to lift up Him that was sent to be the Son of God. Fire shall he breathe upon his enemies, and they shall be consumed with holy fire, and I, God the Lord will be glorified and pleased at this. The times are coming when prophets shall arise to speak their doctrine, and false teachers will arise to teach what they have been taught to persuade the nations, and persuade they will. Be careful not to hear those who speak with sugar coated messages, those who speak more about mammon rather than the True Source. I AM that Source whence all things flow, My children. I hath called many, but few have I chosen, and* those that I have chosen will be that which is called the remnant. They will have immense power never before seen in this day and age, they will seem to appear then disappear and you will not know whence they came. And as My word saith, ' This is that of those that are of the Spirit, like the wind, you know not whence they camest.' I have lifted up many, and by their own hand have they fallen; started in the Spirit but have fallen into the depths of darkness," **saith the Lord of Hosts,** " The glory of the Lord shall be revealed, and in the words of the prophets shall I reveal more of Myself that all nations might know the true God, and have the knowledge of the Spirit of God in them. Those that are hated for righteousness sake theirs is the kingdom of God, those that are meek they shall inherit the world, those that love the Lord their God shall see my Face and I will be glad to see them. For those that despise My doctrine, despise Me, who they say is their God, and I shall despise them when they appear to me in their deaths, and they shall be cast into outer darkness just as My Word saith. For many shall come from different places in the world and sit with Abraham and the forefathers of the children of Israel, but those that are supposed to be children of the kingdom SHALL be casted into outer darkness for they knoweth not Me, the True Light of God, their Savior. Nothing will save you in that day, but only if you had lived by My commandments, had love just as I commanded in your works for Me, and did as I said to will you inherit the kingdom of heaven. Only if you had My Spirit will I recognize thee as one of My children. Many of you deny the power of My Hand, yet you say you know the power of the Holy Ghost! Hypocrites thou art! I have seen your blasphemous claims against those who have inherited the tongues of heaven, and I come in My son to say that if you continue in your denial, you, too will be denied before Me, the Father of heaven! Shake from the shackles that Satan has placed around you! Lay down your pride before My feet that I might crush it under My feet and give you the Confidence and the Faith of God, My children! Nothing shall separate me from the love of God, you say, but through your denial, doubt, and disobedience do you separate yourselves! I AM not a God of confusion, therefore why do you confuse the people? I have given you My Word that you might teach the young people of their Savior, not twist up the peace into chaos that I hath given *them. Why doth thou not serve Me, but your pastors and bishops, and are after their desires and wants rather than Mine? As I said before in old time, 'I AM a Jealous God, He that is called Jealous.' Hear Me when I say that those who serve the image that the Gentiles have created that is supposed to resemble Me will be put to shame. As I said before in old time, ' I AM not glorified in graven images, nor will I give them My praise.' I AM He that hath said this, "Why doth thou ignore what Your Creator saith? Why do you follow the claims of men, rather than Mine? I created and formed you, not your pastors or bishops, I, the Lord, did. He that is called the mighty God is He that formed you, not them." Lift up your eyes to the God of salvation that hath promised you a land full of milk and honey, He that hath called you righteous by the shedding of His Own Blood, the Holy Ghost, the Son and the Father in One Spirit, in One Mind and in One Body as One Person, never three but always One. Those of you that hath known Me hath known My Father also, those that have seen Me hath seen My Father also. Tell Me, bible scholars, how is it physically possible for you to see a son and his father simultaneously, except they be one person? When you look upon the children of the earth they resemble both their fathers and their mothers, and you know that they resemble them because you have seen them and hath compared their looks. But, however, in My Word it states that, 'No man at any point hath seen God.' So, tell Me, I ask, How can thou compare a Son to a Father whom thou hast never seen before? He that looked upon My Son saweth Me, the God and the Father of Heaven, He was the Image of the Invisible God, that if I were to appear without the visible glory of God, you would see My Son. I had to put upon flesh that My children might have beheld Me, and My Word bares witness of this doctrine, 'Father, I pray that these may be One as we are One, that they may be One in Us.' You know the scripture in My Word when it saith, ' The water, the Spirit and the blood bare witness, and these three are One.' My Son is the blood, the soul that was crucified for humanity; the Spirit of He that was in Him which was of the Father, for there is only One Spirit because as My Son declared, ' God is Spirit, so those that worship should worship Him in Spirit and in Truth', and the Word is He that was spoken to come, He that formed the foundation of the world at the beginning, He that is said* to be God in the scriptures. ' In the beginning was the Word, and the Word was with God, and the Word was God. The same was in the beginning with God.' This is He as I had said is to be declared as God according to the scriptures. Hear Me when I saith, that I speaketh as the Father to His Children and I wish that you knew Me that you might be powerful, and edified along with your zeal for Me," **saith the Lord God of heaven and Zion.**

"I, the Father, speaketh, and because I AM God, I must provide the very necessities that you need in order to perform such things that I speak of. I have sent forth many to teach the gospel, but nowadays it's hard to know who is who: who are of Me, and who are full of the devil. This requires great discernment, especially in these last days because as you know there are wolves in sheeps clothing. They hide in plain sight, no one truly being able to notice them and those that do, in the church they are considered a "nobody" and by them saying something about how they feel about a pastor is on a level of "godly blasphemy". Because of their reputation as a prophet, a bishop, a teacher or a minister they are quickly shut down with lies and sabotage. Are these my people? Aren't you supposed to be one in My Son and I? Why do you hate on one another? Why doth thou break the commandment by not loving thy neighbor, or the one that I abhorrest the most, bearing false witness against your brethren? You are no better than the publicans and sinners! You fit right in with the sinners, make sure that they like you by participating in ungodly affairs. I see all of it and those of you who think that you will escape judgment, you should rethink your decisions to do so. Again, I AM not a God of confusion, but peace and if what you are doing in the body is not bringing peace to those who seek understanding in the place of holiness then are you truly doing as I ask? Are you serving Me how I see fit? You are sent to edify not to lie on the pulpit! You sheep out there that have seemed to be overthrown by the false sheep will arise with a shout, a shout so loud that it will destroy those who have seemed to destroy you, and everything that they've built thus far. I prophecy, that by the end of this year everything that they took from you will be restored unto you and them some. You will be overflowing with abundance, everything will be met and you will no longer want for anything. For My

Word saith, ' The Lord is my Shepherd, and I shall not want.' Say this of Me, for I AM He that provides and is providing for you. I wish to do a new thing in your life that you might flourish with grace and become great in the kingdom and great in the land," **saith the Lord God Almighty,** " 'God is good', says men, but why doth thou complain against Me? You say, ' This is the day the Lord has made and I will surely be glad in it,' yet you deny My help in the day that I have made for you, and you wonder why things take a turn because of your lack of faith in Me, My children. Many have turned their backs on Me because of their lack of faith in what they want provided for them. They lack the understanding that they lived, moved, and had their being in Me alone. Their will was no longer was for them, but Mine was and they failed to understand that I have all things in My Hands and that I control all things. Of course I know when and if men's hearts will turn against Me, but it's their choice and I will not force them otherwise, but I will mention to them through particular circumstances on that they should return to Me. If they have no place in Me to begin with, then they will return and stay in their will, but, however, if they have been called and chosen by Me, the Lord, as they began to to turn their hearts from Me they will began to hear that inner voice calling to them and they will listen because I hath given them that ear to hear Me, because I have called them. And they shall return to the Lord, their King, and I shall rejoice with song and sing over them My love for them. For I delighteth greatly in those who seek to know Me, for I AM a just God, and I AM trustworthy, and I can meet all your needs that need to be met. Rest in Me, and know that I AM the Lord, He that provideth and then watch Me work for you, My children. Hear My voice, O My people! For I AM speaking but no one is listening, I AM calling but no one is picking up, the prophets that speak to you that you've chosen to listen to speak nothing but prosperity and how you can receive a new house. I AM not a God that is moved by money, but rather by faith, as I have shown My son, My servant, the author of this very book is that; faith is the currency of heaven. As quick as a cashier is to move when you hand them cash, I AM even quicker when faith is brought before Me. The exchange faith for what you are wanting Me to provide you with can happen quickly, but only if you have faith! No one is willing to go the *extra mile to pray for what it is that you desire, yes, I can send money straight into your bank when you ask, but I'd rather spend time with you in your closet, in your prayer time with Me that we may discuss what you need to do to get there and how to go about doing it."* **saith the Lord God of Israel.** *"Wisdom. That is what many of you need this very day. No one bares this gift, but Me your Father in heaven and I bestow her upon you that you might know how to go about doing your tasks that I have thee to do. Knowledge tells you about the situation, but wisdom tell you how to go about solving the situation! You are sent before wolves in sheep's clothing, snakes who skin is beautiful and desirable to touch! You need this very Wisdom in which I speak of and it comes straight from the kingdom of heaven, right from My throneroom. I send angels before you to speak to you concerning the things that are coming and the things that are already upon you, to edify you that you might be ready for these times. I AM not a God Who confuses, as I have spoken before but I bring peace to those who need it and I bring revelation to those who seek to understand the things of God and His Righteousness. Nothing can be made perfect, nothing can be made whole without Me filling it because I AM perfect and whole, full of all understanding, all knowledge, and all wisdom. I AM sending forth mighty men and women of God to speak such wonders before you that you might understand My Glory, that you might see the power of God. They will speak marvellous things, and shew forth mighty exploits they shall call things into their places right in front of you. Healing will be called through their mouths and it shall be so. They will demonstrate the dominion that I had once given before with Adam and Eve, they shall say, "O mountain, move from your place that the power of God might be shown!" And the power of God will be shewn in front of all the astrologers, the Chaldeans, the evil and wicked hearts, the prideful, the scientists, and the mediums, they will see what true power looks like. They shall be greatly feared by the children of disobedience, every time one falls they shall cheer with a great shout that they are no longer on the earth to torture them with their marvellous works that are from God. They shall see these very things, but instead of turning to Me that will cower in fear, keep their pride, blaspheming My Name because of their lack of understanding. It shall ever increase worse than it has* *ever been since the beginning of the time of man. Men's hearts shall be so vile that it will be called in the last days upon the news network's, " Almost Unbelievable" or "Something from a movie!" Because evil will run rampant upon the earth, and the same land where Christianity lies from it shall it outpour evil into every corner from the earth. It shall even outpour it's own inhabitants, and their bodies shall be found floating in the rivers and oceans due to war and murder. They shall turn upon one another fiercely, causing trust to be a foreign thing in the land. It shall be so bad that it will come to a point to where people shall travel in groups to their local supermarket to ensure safety for one another. Weapons, all weaponry, will be banned by the state government, and anyone not willing to give up their guns and other weapons shall endure great consequences from your government. Many shall be slain in order that all may fall in line, to make sure that the message in the land is clear. There shall be no sort of uprising in the common people for they will bow down to the new leader that will be heavily militarized, heavily guarded, and very strong in his countenance. He shall order this and that and it shall come to him when he calls it. He shall issue an order that all give praise and honor to his god, to himself, that he might be glorified above all else. This will usher in the persecution of the saints of God, the beheading, and the lynching, and the scourging of My people. Many shall turn from the faith at the knowledge of this, they will even give up his or her brother or sister. This will be the separation among the saints, and those who aren't truly for Me and My doctrine they will be shown before the land as heroes for giving up their brothers and sisters. They will tell them that they have done a good thing, but My Hand will be against them, and they will be under My Heel just those who serve the enemy in those times. I warn, and I plead with you, My Church, yet you do not pay attention to My warnings! you act as though everything is fine, and that nothing is about to take place. You say, " I have time, I don't need to worry about this and that, because God will take care of me." The issue with that My children is that you don't seek Me so that you might stay close to Me that you might remain in My graces, within My love, within My protection, My people. I need you to understand that I am God, and that will keep you if you want to be kept. If you do not pray and seek Me* for a particular thing that I will not move, because "ye have not because ye ask not." Ask and ye shall receive what it is that you need and want. I AM a God Who loves to provide in different ways for My people that they may tell of their God and Who He is that I may be glorified in them and by them," **saith the God of heaven,** " Nothing makes me happier than to see My creation moving and prospering in the way that I would have them. I make things new for them everyday; new mercies, new graces, new blessings, new love, new peace, new wisdom, and new knowledge. I have many things planned for those who wish to serve and seek to please Me, their Lord. I AM glad when My people are quick to glorify Me, and worry not about self-exposure, but they keep Me in the place of glorification that I have placed in their hearts for Me. They see that I deserve glorification and adoration, they lift Me up as their King, God, and Lord, the One Who is called Jesus Christ, the mighty God. I AM He that founded and created the earth He that called everything good and saw that it was good," **saith the Lord Jesus, the God of Zion and Power,** "I AM the same that was in the beginning with God, and as My Word states, " In the beginning was the Word, and the Word was God, and the Word was God. The same was in the beginning with God," then I go onto say through my prophet, John the Baptist, that, " the Word became flesh and dwelt among us." I AM the same yesterday, today, and forever. My Word in Hebrews chapter thirteen states that I AM the same that was with God and that was God, My Children. Understand that the prophetic visions that were given before My manifestation into the earthly realm were clearly presented to showcase that I, God, would come on the earth that I might save you and restore you back to My Image. In which I created you by in the beginning of time. Never underestimate My power, for I AM not a God that is bound by chains, nor AM I a God that can be halted or stopped because I AM invincible and full of almighty power and authority, no one can override what I have done or spoken, I AM the Ultimate Authority in the heavens and in the earth," **says the LORD.** " Understand O My People, that I called thee by My Name and nothing that proceedeth out of My mouth shall return unto Me void. I know who I hath called and whom I have chosen. I know who will remain with Me in the end, I know who will endure the hard times *that I endured when I came upon the earth. You may ask, "Why would God, Who is loving, allow us or wants us to endure such hardship?" First, I AM God, and I have commanded these things to be so, if you are not of the Spirit these such things terrify you, and push you towards the sugar coated beliefs that everything will be fine that there are no changes that need to be made, because you are perfect how I made you. I make things new, I don't form things into a thing of old, but when I step in all things inside of you and around you become new by My lovingkindness and grace that is given from My hand. Only those willing to bare the cross of My Son, will enter the gates of heaven, and I know who I have selected and I know who will endure till the end of time! When I shall intervene on your behalf and take you into glory. Trust Me that if I was with My Son, I shall surely be with thee until the end of time," says the Lord of Hosts and Power, the One Who was, is, and is to come in the glory as of the only begotten of the Father, the One and Only Son, Jesus the Almighty Christ! Amen!*

The Lord promised protection in such days. As Daniel had seen and spoken about us in that time, *"And such as do wickedly against the covenant shall he corrupt by flatteries: but the people that do know their God shall be strong, and do exploits." (Daniel 11:32, KJV)* So all this, everything that I have written from the Lord thus far is highly important! It's important to all those who consider themselves, *Christians*, and who supposedly *"have the Spirit of God" living inside them.* Those who know Jesus Christ will know that I have been sent by Him to preach His Gospel that the True God might be known through me. That the Mediator between God and man, was the God that sent Him to Himself to *be* the Mediator for us. We should be able to gather and see this, "

[38] For I am persuaded, that neither death, nor life, nor angels, nor principalities, nor powers, nor things present, nor things to come,

[39] Nor height, nor depth, nor any other creature, shall be able to separate us from the love of God, which is in Christ Jesus our Lord.

That God no longer wanted anything separating us from Him. He no longer *needed nor wanted* a Mediator other than Himself, so, He came Himself to be the Mediator that we may be truly and fully reconciled to our Creator in Heaven who is Jesus the Living Christ and Lord! Amen!

God is amazing and truly deserves to be praised on the highest! Because a Holy King clothed in such majesty came down from Heaven, the place where He resided, and lived as King in all His apparel that He might save a wretch and vile people as ourselves! We cannot continue to be silent in these evil and terrifying days, the world needs us to step out for God that they too might be saved! The world awaits the manifestation for the sons(and daughters) of God to arise and do what we are called to do!(*Romans 8:19, KJV.) So let us arise with a shout of victory unto our King Who sits high upon the throne! That as we go forward in the name of God, we have in mind that we are more than conquerors through Him that loved us before the foundation of the earth! JESUS! We love You, Jesus! We come that we might bless your Holy Name and lift You High, bring tidings to Your Throne, that we may remain at Your Feet, and continue our walk in the Spirit with You, O Holy God and King! Selah!*

WARNING: Brothers and sisters, whomever is reading this book, if you are on the fence struggling to believe, or not truly sure that you even want to serve Christ. This next chapter is not for you, but for the Church of God, the True Believers who understand the events that are upon us, because you read of the Truth, you will then be held accountable to bear it, to share it, and to warn others of the coming devastation and darkness. God bless you, and I hope that those of you who read it draw yourself closer to the Lord Jesus Christ, and to His Son that was, is, and is to come again, Amen.

12. Church

God always said, " Seek and ye shall find. Knock and the door shall be opened to you." I have sought God concerning such heavenly matters, concerning the end of days, and what is has to do with God's people. I have now understood my duty as a man of God to spread the Gospel of Jesus Christ the Lord and God, the King of Israel, the Just One Who was and is, Who is the Righteousness of God, JESUS. I am called by His Name to go throughout the land to demonstrate the power of God, only through and by the Spirit of Jesus Christ, for I am His servant and His son. We as the Church, the true children of God are called by His Name and are distinct from those who claim to be God's chosen but are not. We are peculiar in every way, and we are of a royal priesthood, set aside for the righteousness and holiness of God the Lord of Hosts and Glory! Lord you get the glory out of our lives, and is the One Who called each and everyone of us to be. We praise you O Heavenly Father for not what You've done, but just simply for Who You are, a loving God and Holy King, clothed in Grace and Power, a Man of Righteousness and Valor, saturated in Holiness that comes from You alone, O Jesus thou Son of the Living God! Amen.

This is the formation of the Church, this is the foundation of the ones who are called Christians. This whole book was sent forth to anoint, to spread, to reach the four corners of the earth that men might see who Jesus Christ truly is and fall down and worship Him before the time of His return. That His Grace might cover those who blasphemed His Name, those who made sure to put a snare down for His people to trap them, to set them free from the bondage of sin and the yoke of darkness.

God is still good spite the evil that is added to His Name by those who hate Him, He is still God spite of their blasphemous claims and accusations. He doesn't not need to be validated by ANY man for Him to be God. God came upon the earth in the form a servant, fashioned Himself like a man, made Himself of no reputation even though He was more than deservant of the praise, glory, and honor. He stepped into the earthly realm as God and was God before the day of His birth, and was STILL even God when He died for the ransom for many. I say to those that have understood my speech in the Holy Ghost, who is our Spiritual Rabbi, rejoice in the Lord, in the Spirit for He has given you what no man can find nor unlock, but only if He gives you the key, which is Himself. I praise God that He sits on the throne of Glory, that He is simply the I AM, even the I AM before the day of Abraham was. I thank God for His Son, for His Spirit, and for His Glory that was bestowed upon the earth in His earthly ministry. I thank Jesus for His Servant that was sent to bear the sins of those who hated Him, that instead of Him giving up He said for me and all others that are willing to come to Him, those who will acknowledge Him as their Savior and God, "Nevertheless." Hallelujah, glory be to God the Father, the Son, and the Holy Ghost, Amen. Thank You Heavenly Father Jesus the Living and Almighty God!

Going forward in the name of the Father, and of the Son, and of the Holy Ghost I will now show you in scripture some of the things that God has revealed to me in the prophecies He has given me for the times that are coming. I pray that ye seek God concerning the prophecies that I share with you, go to the throne of God seeking His face concerning such information. For I know that these words are straight from the mouth of the King, the One Who is called God the Holy One. The words I speak concerning Him cannot be anything but the truth, for if the words I spoke weren't of Him, my death would be imminent, and He would deal with me justly in a holy manner in which I should deserve. But by His Grace He has lifted me up in heavenly places with my Savior and God, Jesus Christ. He is my Friend through the faith of God, and we have a relationship in which we speak daily to one another in secret. "The things that are done in secret will be awarded in the public eye," said the

Lord in His earthly ministry. And because I have done these things in the name of the Lord Jesus Christ, He has begun to reward me by His Hand and has elevated Me to the place that is needed in the physical as well as the spiritual. I thank Thee O God for Your continued love, peace, joy, and understanding when I have fallen, and done wrong. You held me close when I should have been casted into outer darkness where there is weeping and gnashing of teeth. Yet You covered with me Your Grace and held me together with Your Lovingkindness, Amen, O God of Zion, and Hallelujah be to Your Holy Name, Selah!

Prophecy One

These words that are about to be brought forth might terrify you, even might cause you to think about some things, but as I said before pray unto the Lord for clarification upon these prophecies that were given from Him that He might expand your thinking to understand such things. So here is what the Lord of Armies showed unto me in a dream when I was asleep. I saw this November 2nd, 2018, on a Friday. I will write it as I have it written in my journal that I keep for the Lord's holy words.

Last night I had a dream about the antichrist! I saw what he looked like and he had an accent, and he was planning things, but he wasn't in "office" or public yet, but he was planning schemes. In the dream I said it wasn't him, but from a movie, but I think it ended up being him. I was really close to his face, hearing what he was saying, he looked like a normal man, but I knew he was evil!

He looked lifeless, you could tell in his eyes, but only from the Spirit because from the outside he looked like a normal man, but things began to happen after that, tribulation I want to say. It was immediate. There was a close up to his eyes and he looked evil and then he smiled then it went away. THE BLOOD OF JESUS! Over my family and myself! He was a white male, light brown hair, blue eyes, looked young, in his twenties or thirties, probably for sure thirties. I can't remember his plans, but I remembered exactly what he looked like and that it was him.(but it's sort of a good thing because we're almost to the glory with the LORD!)

"Don't worry nor be afraid son, you will conquer him, just as I have conquered him," saith the Lord Jesus! Hallelujah! Thank You, Lord, Amen!

I think that he's already here, but he's waiting to make his move! Or that he is about to make a move! I saw him in an attire that is similar to running for office, and he was sitting at a desk(Daniel 11:27, KJV)in an office. I saw people around him and he was talking to them about his plans. It makes sense because of all this corruption and evil running rampant in the world!

ASSASSINATION

The Lord has shown me this in the spirit, and I must pray, as a man of God, over our president that is in office. He will come at a time when everything is crazy and chaotic so he can be seen as the "Peace Maker between the countries"(the Lord showed me this as a headline in a newspaper, or a digital newspaper). He will be seen as a savior to the people, but he will be evil incarnated and far from spreading peace, My son. Beware with your prophetic eyes son, his emergence into the spotlight.

President Donald Trump will get into office again and this will cause a major uproar in the people of America and it will cause major villany even attacks on those who support him, even death, also I see attacks and threats on the white house, bombings, but they will fail. Until the emergence of Satan, the evil incarnate he will destroy with a flame all that is called civilization, and build a new world above the ashes of the American dream and the world. He will have demands and armies to ensure that his demands are met. No one will dare to come against him,(as in the white house) an assassination attempt will try to happen(but the people) but it will end badly. The people that he will blame will be Christians and this will commence the destruction and the tribulations, and the martyrs of God's people. This man will try to uproot the Word of God(Daniel Chapter 7:20-28 & 11:30-40 KJV) from the earth, will have seemed to smother the Lights of God, but then will emerge a people, a remnant of God's people that he hasn't had a chance to touch, because God has kept them by His Grace and Mighty Hand!!

He will grow very angry and try to wipe them out, but God will cause them to be a standard against him and just like the woman who grew wings and flew when the enemy came like a flood so will the people and they will escape with great power and might by the Mighty Hand of the Lord Jesus Christ.

He will constantly try to cause people to perceive him as good and innocent when he is truly evil and ruthless! God will show him to be a dictator and a manipulator. Trump will be missed in office when the man steps in office... then office or throne will be claimed, stolen by him after he has murdered the president that God has placed. His death will be significant to believers. He will try to reassure the people of America that he means well even though he changes everything, including the history of America(Daniel 7:23-24). He will then claim to be God as the Word states after sitting in the temple, in the temple of God(Daniel 9:27, KJV) The American Embassy will be the bridge for him to emerge as the 'little horn' to the holy place. He will devour them murderously and no one shall be able to stop him but the people of God, and God Himself in these days!

" I gave you this for purpose son, because everything that I had you to write will happen exactly that way your wrote it. You will remember these words in which I spoke to you concerning this, and I will have you to release it to America and you will be known as a prophet," thus saith the LORD of lords, and the King of kings! Amen! Thank You Sweet JESUS! Hallelujah! Thank You God the Most High King! Amen LORD!

The people the Lord speaks of He saith they shall go forth conquering and conquering and going forth to conquer in Jesus Name, Amen!

And I just wanted to mention by the Holy Ghost that the Father had spoken these words to me prior me going to the Word for clarification to ensure that it was actually in the Word of God, but the Word God which is Jesus Christ can only expound and speak on Who He is what He has already spoken in His Word anything but His Word is not to be listened to. The Father in Heaven has blessed me, and now you with *such heavenly knowledge. Now it shall spread across the globe like wildfire and many of you will recall the words that were written here in this very book. Some that did not heed the warning before you read the chapter will sorely afraid and terrified because it will then be too late and will not have done what the Father had commanded you to do by sharing the gospel of Jesus Christ to the poor in spirit, the things that everyone should know about the times, and about their God, and what He has planned and how He will save us in the end. And He, that is called Jesus Christ the Holy One, the God and the Lord of creation will be sitting upon the judgement seat to judge your actions and the things that you did not do. I am only a messenger of God, and whether you believe that or not I am here to speak His Word, Amen!*

Prophecy Two

The word of the Lord came unto me January 13th, 2019. The word of the Lord saith, " After the eagle has fallen, there shall be another image that will arise that will exude: strength, power, fierceness, and intellect. It will grown and strive greatly arising like the little horn in Daniel. He will be great in the eyes of men, he will be skilled in logistics, science, he will be very intelligent in seemingly all things. He will even know the word of God, will seemingly teach on the word of God, but his underlying theme and desire will be to destroy. He will issue a state warning, a global warning to serve this new image after he has gotten the trust of the American Embassy, the British, all the great powers of the earth, he will then wipe clean all things that were before and set up his empire, that he will say that has been building in his family for a millenia. He will be so trusted, so loved that everyone will bow down to his image, and hear his name that will be of old and of evil nature. 666. This is the reason why I showed you the numbers son before you went back to sleep! I AM warning you so that you can warn other of the coming corruption and evil. That the knowledge of a one world power is not a conspiracy, but has been foretold, and is slowly emerging. That talk of there being super soldiers will come into play, but they will be satanically and demonically possessed. It will be something no one has ever seen. They will be issued by him and only by him, he will encourage them to follow(countries and powers) his lead, that he will supply everything that they need to protect them from you, the naysayers, or the evil ones, those who oppose his leadership and from the mouth of those who worship him; his excellency.

Science will rule, and his science will dominate all things, his genetically evolved supplements will cause healing, healing from cancerous cells, sexually transmitted, broken bones, torn off limbs and ligaments will regrow instantly through his sciences. He will call it, " A New Era of Science," says the Lord of hosts! "But to the people that serve Me he will be issuing out demonically inspire pills to deceive and falsely heal. You will be like a pain in his side, every time he breathes you will speak a word against him, but no one will listen. He will tell the people that all he is trying to achieve is peace, but in that same moment he will be destroying and uprooting all that was before just as the book of Daniel speaks of, and you will broadcast this My son, you will let the people know beforehand and as this unfolds they will bow down to Me, their Savior, and confess Me as Lord before it's too late. For he will come but you will be long ready for him before he comes, My son." saith The Lord of hosts! Amen! And Glory to the Lamb of the Living God! God has given me a warning and I must warn the people! The Lord of the Sabbath gave me an analogy of someone who will be tried for righteousness sake!

Almost like a man who got a football scholarship he will have to endure certain hardships, have to really work hard, and go through them to ensure that he truly want what they received. Amen! God is good and merciful! I praise Him for His glorious words of warnings, understanding, and clarification because there is much that the church nowadays has never heard, so many things that we question as a body and I believe that the God of heaven and earth has chosen me to be one of the many voices arising in the Spirit for Truth and Justice for Righteousness and Holiness sake! Hallelujah Praise God!

<u>A word from the Lord concerning the demon of Abortion</u>

"This is important, My son. The spirit of Molech has been released in the land. He is a king that once ruled, a god to the Ammonite people, who took their child, given to him by those in darkness. But, I, the God of Jacob and Israel, hath brought life against the power and stronghold of Molech, although his name is no longer, Molech, but he has changed his name to fit the agenda of his people, Abortion. Every time there is an abortion there is a sacrifice given to the spirit of Molech. Evil has run rampant and has been unleashed in the world, and within the walls of the United States, where I once resided, but no longer do, for I have removed Myself, from the presence of men whose hearts and fists has risen up against Me. As you say son, I AM a Gentleman, and only go where I AM welcomed. Death has been given power by the inhabitants of earth, they no longer want life to thrive but rather have darkness instead of Me." says the Lord. (Leviticus 20:2-5.) " I AM sending Word through to warn the saints of God, to warn the people of the land that the deaths of their children are sacrifices given unto the god of the Ammonites, the spirit of Molech, whose desire is death and their children. For the worship of other gods has already been enacted, so, I the True God of the earth must expose them that they may be known and the people might turn from their wicked ways unto Me, the God of Life, Joy, and Peace," saith the Lord God of Power! Thank You, O Lord, for Your grace and peace, and Your Holy Word straight from Heaven and Your Throneroom! Amen! Hallelujah! The Lord also added, " Molech was the abomination of the Ammonites, some were Jewish people, and they worshipped him and sacrifice their children, to the god, Molech," says the Lord from Zion. Amen!

[10] The thief cometh not, but for to steal, and to kill, and to destroy: I am come that they might have life, and that they might have it more abundantly.(John 10:10, KJV.)

The devil's desire is to try and destroy what God has given, to corrupt what God has put forth. Notice how everyone in "the left"are against all the things pertaining to life, for they are the children of disobedience and their father is from below, the devil. For Satan wishes to wipe clean the *things of God and begin his world but the True Father of heaven, Jesus Christ, will crush him under His Heel, and put him where he belongs, in the depths of hell being tortured forever and ever, Amen. Praise God for His Power that is found in His Son only, the Son of Man, who is also called the Son of God, and those that truly know Him, the mighty God and Wonderful Counsellor, Hallelujah Amen!*

A Word from the Lord concerning the spirit of Jezebel.

 The God Who answers by fire is the One we should serve. That is the God of Israel, Jacob, and Abraham(1 Kings 18:19-45, KJV.)
 "Jezebel, comes to destroy the church, spiritually speaking. If she can weaken those around her she will eventually consume them. She killed many of My Prophets, and today she s as well through many that have inherited that spirit. They are set out to dismantle, uproot, strong rooted churches. Spiritually speaking, she will also try to scatter the flock with different interpretations, she knows is wrong just to confuse the flock. She comes as a goat covering her horns, to try and blend in with the flock. When she is settled and every one of the sheep has been deceived then will she show her horns and devour the flock. Do not run as Elijah did, but trust Me and call on My Name. For I AM greater and stronger than Jezebel, she cannot beat Me for I AM the God of Strength, the LORD of Hosts. I will protect My people, My sheep from her so that she will not be able to dig her horns into your sides. Keep watch for her, she will try to appear. Will you run or stand and fight in My Name, and call on Me to reign fire on your enemies? Amen." says the LORD of Hosts! Selah! Amen!

A Word from the Lord Jesus' Heart to His Church

 The Word of the LORD came unto me saying, " My son! Listen! For I have much to tell you! Bring all worries, and stresses, and lay them at My feet, My son, for many things are coming! Destruction, devastation, more cruelty, hide in My Presence. Live in "the shelter of the Most High." For I AM your Protection in the last days, hearken unto My Voice, and lean only on Me! No on devices, family, friends, no one, but Me! Call upon Me son, and I will hear you, and I will come unto you and rescue you. Fear not, for I AM the King of Battle, and I AM Victorious, every time!

The days will turn into darkness, many people will search for the Light, but never find it. Because they seek not Me, but a light that cannot save them. I AM the only One that can save, for I AM mighty to save anyone who asks Me to save them! Like I said son they will seek not Me, the Light, but a false light that cannot save them, a light whose power and light has gone out. I call out to them son, yet they do not listen, son. My Church is losing its ear towards Me, son, and they are now listening only to the pastors! And prophets who have a lying tongue! They have grown to be comfortable in the lies, lies that they know to be lies so that they can remain in darkness. Sin is spreading in the Church son, and I AM calling those truly have My Light in them to speak to the Churches.

I will give warning, but if they do not heed to My Words they will be cut off. Because they are growing no fruit! Nor do they bare a seed! Those that have entered the Church only come to cause division and confusion, but I AM sending you, and others to preach the unadulterated Word of God, My Gospel! My Spirit is being pushed out the church's son! Then, they go off a familiar spirit instead of My Holy Spirit! For My Word says son, " For there will come a time when will not endure sound doctrine."

And the time is here. The Church has turned in to the harlot, she has stepped out on Me several times, looks not to come back to Me, but to divorce Me. She has found someone better, someone with reputation in the church and the world, Barabbas. He is a man that does not offer My bride anything, but death and destruction. My Church! My Bride! Come back to Me! Before it's too late! I AM your Husband, your Bridegroom! Do not consummate with Barabbas, for the son you will bear will be of destruction and famine, and of devastation! I call to you over and over yet you do not listen! Come back to Me! Return to Me! Fall back into My arms!

Return! My love for you has not grown cold nor bitter for My love for you still burns for you! I love you son, preach the Gospel of My Son, Jesus Christ; unprocessed, unadulterated, Word of God to all nations and all over this country," saith the LORD of Immense Grace!

¹ I charge thee therefore before God, and the Lord Jesus Christ, who shall judge the quick and the dead at his appearing and his kingdom;

² Preach the word; be instant in season, out of season; reprove, rebuke, exhort with all longsuffering and doctrine.

³ For the time will come when they will not endure sound doctrine; but after their own lusts shall they heap to themselves teachers, having itching ears;

⁴ And they shall turn away their ears from the truth, and shall be turned unto fables.

⁵ But watch thou in all things, endure afflictions, do the work of an evangelist, make full proof of thy ministry. (2 Timothy 4:1-5, also read about the Lord, and his heart is also seen in Matthew 27:11-54. He did it without question for you, why do ye question the hardship that we should go through for Him? He is our God and Savior! HALLELUJAH JESUS MY GOD AND CREATOR!)

God is preparing His True Church for the trials and tribulations that we should endure for Him, for Righteousness sake! Those who only have inherited the Spirit of God through the baptism of His Son shall they be called the children of God. Because He saith in His Word that when we are baptized in the name of Jesus, the Father when send the Holy Ghost in His Name! As we spoken before that the Holy Ghost comes with tongues, you cannot have the Holy Ghost and no tongues, because Jesus is He that is spoken in John, " He that will baptize you in fire(in the Holy Ghost)." (John 1:33, KJV.) There is life in His Name, and if we believe in His name we shall receive life, and our spirits shall raise from the bondage of death and sin, arising with Christ in the heavenly places through the Spirit of Christ Who is the Holy Ghost. For John 1 saith, "¹² But as many as received him, to them gave he power to become the sons of God, even to them that believe on his name:

[13] Which were born, not of blood, nor of the will of the flesh, nor of the will of man, but of God."

Look closely at verse twelve, "....to them he gave power to become the sons of God, even to them that believe on His Name." So just by you believing on His Name alone could bring you into the family of God, because by you acknowledging the name of Jesus, you are acknowledging God the Father who is the Son. You are believing the report of God, and on His Holy Name that it is mighty to save you from your sin and circumstance! Amen! Hallelujah! God is sending word to you to let you know that He has heard your calling out to Him and that if you believe He will happily save you with delight! God delights in those He loves, and trust me He loves you my friends. I thank You, O God, you never cease to amaze me, and I know that throughout this book you will touch many, and You and only You, Jesus my God will get the glory out of it all! O Glorious Father and Savior. I love you, Jesus Christ, You are mine, and I am Yours and I am glad to be Yours O God! No matter that hate and the ridicule that comes with the publication of this book, as long as You get the glory I shall rest easy in Your Name and in Your Arms! I say it again, O God, I am glad to be called a man of the Most High, a man of God, and a follower of Jesus Christ the Messiah and God the Father, Amen! Be glorified, O God that sits on the throne of glory, O Lord of heaven and earth!

God is a God that loves to help prepare us for what is to come in the end, this is what we have to overcome to be in the glory of God! Isn't He worth it? Ask yourselves! Is Jesus, the Son of God, who was revealed to be the Image of the Invisible God, worth the harassment-before you began to find a way out of it, and try to make it about you, recall what He did for you, YOU WERE WORTH IT! God stripped Himself of visible glory for us who once not had a desire to approach Him, but at one point wanted to remain in darkness. He died for those of us who used to be liars, gossipers, full of hate and clothed in self-inflicted shame! Reconcile yourselves unto Him in Jesus Name! Only through baptism in Jesus Name shall you receive the righteousness of God, and for you to be truly cleansed, God will baptize you in His Holy Fire, removing the wrinkles and stains of sin through the blood of Jesus Christ. For those of you who go over the gate rather than through the door and called by the Lord, " robbers and thieves," because you come to take things that were not given to you. You claim an inheritance that your name is not found upon, you have said, " I am a child of the Most High," yet you have no Holy Ghost to support that claim. You say, " God spoke to me concerning this.." how can you say that you have heard God, when He has no place in you to speak? You doubt His power through tongues, you've been preaching for fifty-plus years, yet you still don't have the full revelation of Jesus Christ the Son of God along with the Holy Ghost and tongues. There is a mixed multitude here Church! We cannot move as a body because we are simply serving different Gods! The God I serve answers through fire, the next persons god answers without a clear voice, the next answers according to your feelings rather than his own spirit. Which one shall we serve? Which God has not limits to where I cannot contain Him, Who can expound through His Spirit, through His Word and with clear words a direction through His own mouth. The God that answers by fire is the One that I chose because I follow Him, He doesn't follow me. I'd rather die than have a god that goes off of my feelings and MY might rather than his own spirit.

This God that I speak of He is even called, Wonderful, the mighty God, Counsellor, the Prince of Peace, the Everlasting Father, which of these titles sounds like a God that I can put in a box? None. Jesus is the Creator of this earth and the heavens up above, and He is the Same that came and devoured my enemies even when I knew not that I had enemies. He is the Same yesterday, today and forever(Hebrews 13:8, KJV), He is the Same that was in the beginning with God(John 1:2,KJV), He is the One that was the Word made flesh(John 1:14, KJV), He went from being spacious and vast into bodily form for me. He asked me not if I thought it was okay, but within His Own Counsel(Isaiah 11:1-4) did He decide what would be best for me(Jeremiah 29:11). That He should clothed Himself in that of man(Philippians 2:7-8), that He be God in the flesh, to die as a Man and yet at the same time conquer death with His Life(1 Corinthians 15:54-57)! I thank God through the Lord Jesus Christ that He is One God, in One Body, in One Spirit that I should live by, I thank thee O God that I have the Spirit of Christ that I may be called one of His. (Romans 8:9, KJV.) And nothing can separate me from Your Love, Your protection, Your peace, Your understanding, Your Grace and Lovingkindness. I thankful to You. O Jesus thou Son of God, and to You am I thankful to Only because through you I have the Father, and only through You can I see Him and one day behold Him. You are the Righteousness of God, therefore I shall follow you all the days of my life, even though it be a vapor of smoke, I shall live this moment for You, O God for You, the lover of my soul and life are truly worth the pain and the wait O Holy One of God. You are so precious to me, gold and silver will never amount to a touch or just a glance from you because in you do I find my life, because with you I find my Strength to say, "To God be the glory," even in the baddest of times. You give me strength O God, for you Joy covers me from head to toe and nothing can bring me down, no shame, no hate, no demon in hell, no angel in heaven, no power, no principality, no earthly power shall separate me from your joy, love, power and peace, O mighty God of Zion! Nothing! Thank You, O Jesus thou Son of God, my Father in heaven Who sits upon the throne of glory, who is called the Lord of glory, who was crucified for me which should have been a murderer's(Barabbas')death, but You O God were the giver of Life, not the destroyer thereof! Thank You, O Mighty God of Promises! You art good, thou art good, O Father of lights! Mighty God you have saved billions just by the stripes that were on Your back, with each drop of blood a leper was cleansed, there was a mother who was given back her wayward son, with each limp was there a father reconciled to his daughter. With each stripe we were healed! Hallelujah!(Isaiah 53: 3-5, KJV.) Praise God!

This word from the Lord Jesus was given unto me Monday, September 25th, 2017.

While I was sleeping, somewhat awake, aware in my hearing. I heard the voice of the LORD tell me, "Ezekiel 4:17, go to Ezekiel 4:17!" (Please go read!)

" The land will go bare. It will not produce crops, nor will the cattle give birth to their calfs. No one will know how this came to be, but

those that had an ear to hear, and a mind to receive will understand this predicament, this famine. For too long now, I have allowed sin to be upon this world; and those that grow, they give no thanks nor honor to the One that has given this to them!

I AM going to swipe away all crops, every inch, every trace of it until there's NOTHING left! Not until they figure out Who gave it to them. I AM finally giving them what they deserve, I AM finally cutting off the goods that come from evil. Through this some will see, and recognize that only, I, God, the Christ, Who is the giver, and taker of things. "The LORD giveth, and the LORD taketh away. Blessed be the name of the LORD." There will be a sudden decrease in all things: cattle, corn, wheat, fruit, vegetables, cotton, oil, and gas. These things will increasingly run out due to sin. You think that these earthquakes, tsunamis, floods are something there is more to come to those who haven't repented! This is why it is so important that you tell people to repent! Death will come, sweeping away families, firstborn, little ones, because of sin that families, heads of government, parents have allowed!

Death will be imminent, it will be so sudden that people will think that it is some pandemic, some experiment, that NASA, had put in the atmosphere, and it went wrong. Protests will get more, and more violent, until there will be "wars", shootouts between civilians, killing one another, brutally. This world will get worse and worse before I return, but whoever lives under the shelter of the Most High, shall abide under the shadow of the Almighty.

North Korea, will eventually come through on their promises. They will rain what will seem to be "hell-fire" on the United States. Pray for the soldiers those in the armies, in all branches, they need it! The death toll be at large, eventually they will stop counting and guesstimate the total. Loved ones will be lost, the streets will seemed to be paved with blood from commotions in the street, and also there will be much blood in the field. The end will seem that it has come, but it hasn't, there is more, much more will come after this! Make Me your Stronghold! Not your family, friends, acquaintances, people you think you can hold onto because there will be such a corrupt, such a desire to save one's own life that there will be no time to help one another.(This will be their thought process.) Pastors and bishops, those in ministry will their families, and congregants to save their own lives, they will die.(Caught in the crosshairs of destruction.)

Be not afraid, nor saddened, for I will uphold those who will have hearkened to My voice. Just remain in that "secret place." PRAY, REPENT, AND TRUST!" saith the Lord and the God of Foreknowledge and Preparation, He that sits high on the throne and sees all and He is called the Father and is Wonderful, and Whose eyes are everywhere that no one can hide from Him, Amen!

Here's what Ezekiel 4:17 states, ' "[17] That they may want bread and water, and be astonished one with another, and consume away for their iniquity." Even sixteen, so that you may no longer doubt these words from the Lord, but that you might believe that His Words rest in me and speaks to you. Because without the word of God these words would have no validation, because whatever God speaks it mustn't deter from His Holy Word. Amen Jesus!

16, ' "[16] Moreover he said unto me, Son of man, behold, I will break the staff of bread in Jerusalem: and they shall eat bread by weight, and with care; and they shall drink water by measure, and with astonishment:(I wanted to

remind you of the words the Lord Jesus our God gave me, "No one will know how this came to be, but those that had an ear to hear, and a mind to receive will understand this predicament, this famine."

We will understand as His people that this was His doing! And that we are to be dependent on Him and that He as our Lord our Supreme Ruler will surely take care of all things concerning us, Amen. I want to say that I am not trying to scare you into doing what you should ALREADY be doing, but I am just giving you the words of the Lord that you may be prepared in the Spirit by God through His Spirit, Amen.

God has given us the greatest gift, and that is ability to learn, to be able to be taught. As people of God we can get lazy when it comes to studying the word of God for ourselves. We lean on the pastors, so-called-prophets and apostles way too much. Then, not only that the prophets that we listen to don't speak the truth, but prophesy things to get you to buy his next book, or come to his next seminar in which God is not welcomed(the True God that is, Jesus Christ, the Living Word of God, the Word that perceives and knows the intents of men, and calls it out despite their position in the church). Tell me, would you rather allow an epidemic to consume everyone when you have the vaccine, or use the vaccine to cure everyone? Having the Word of God is literally like having the cure for cancer, the right medication to remove the tumor for your skull. Because God is the Creator, He can cure you from ANY disease that you may be carrying, because He formed you in the womb of your mother, and knew you before your parents knew you. The doctors don't know you like God knows you, so don't allow them to tell you that this or that cannot be healed or removed. Praise God for His Graces, for His Mercies, and for His Unconditional Love, and I pray that this book helps you both physically AND spiritually. Also, that it helps you to see that God loves you, and wants you to understand His nature, to understand His love and friendliness that He presents before you.

I thank God for His continual grace that He has shown toward me, His servant and son. I am not perfect by any means, nor have I completed my work in the Kingdom of God upon the earth, but this is only the beginning for me. I pray that when you have completed this book, yes, in its entirety that it fuels you to go out and labor for the Lord God with all fire fueled from the Holy Ghost, with the all the knowledge of the fullness of the Son of the Living God. That you go forward with the anointing to break chains, pull down strongholds, to cast out devils, to heal and set free those who have been broken and beaten down by sin, and help them to rise up once again in and with the Strength of God the Almighty Father of heaven and earth, Amen. God bless you, and see you soon in the name of the Almighty Father, the Matchless Prince the Son of God, and the Blessed Spirit of God the Holy Ghost, in the name of the Mighty Jesus Christ, Amen and Amen, Praise God for His Counsel and Great Wisdom!

ACKNOWLEGDEMENTS

I must, without a doubt give a huge thanks and praise offering to, Jesus Christ, the mighty God of salvation and justice, then to my lovely parents, Roy and Janice Irving. And lastly a special thanks to my late Grandmother, Mary Louise Dickson, the memory of you will never fade. Love you all,

-Jordan M. Irving

A special prayer
(pray with me O powerful saints of God, that He might get the glory!

Father, You reign in heaven and also you dwell in the earth. You have already heard before I have spoken. I pray unto you, the Lord of harvest, that You will send out many laborers into the earth that You might glorified. You said the harvest is plentiful as I plant the seed that You given me to plant, let it spread like wildfire in the earth. Let the fire be unquenchable and uncontained, for You cannot be contained O God, so let not these words you have given me contained. The Spirit of Your Son, Jesus, dwells in us, the hope of glory, get the glory out of my life through this very book O God! Be pleased with me, O Lord, your son and servant. You know that I will cast down my own name so that Your Name might be glorified! For Your word states O Heavenly King that, " For the earth shall be filled with the knowledge of the glory of the Lord, as the water covers the sea," so let it be so O God, Amen! (Habbakuk 2:14)

This book follows the King James Version Bible, I was guided in my Word using the "Scofield Study Bible" as my biblical source for the scriptures, but God gave the meanings behind them, Amen.

Extra Words of encouragement unto the saints

You've completed the book! Yay! Hallelujah! I am so happy that you wanted to even read my book let alone buy it. I am truly grateful to God for His endless mercy and undying faithfulness! *Jesus thou art worthy of all the praise, honor, and glory!* I want to encourage you by the Holy Ghost that no matter what happens in these next couple of years, whatever law they try to bring forth against the people of God, know that Jesus is with you until the end of time. He will never abandon you, but

He is closer than a brother or a mother. He is even closer than your best friend who you tell all your secrets to! God is our Protector and He will keep us from all manner of evil, accusations, negativity, threats against our lives etc. the favor God will cover your from head to toe. Continue to spread the message of Jesus Christ without fear of men, or what they will do unto you if you speak, *speak regardless.* God will walk right alongside of you just He did with His Son, Christ Jesus, and will give you strength to endure the tribulations that come with serving Him.

2 Timothy 1:7 says, *⁷ For God hath not given us the spirit of fear; but of power, and of love, and of a sound mind.*

So, God has called us to work out of love, and out of power, and for our mind to be sound. *What does it mean "to have a sound mind?"* The Holy Ghost revealed to me that when a room is empty sound can travel easily, but when there are things occupying a room sound doesn't travel as fast because it has to try to get *through* the objects. Let me break it down even more, worry, stress, misunderstandings at your job, anger, all manner of sin, fear, etc. are occupying the space of your mind! The sound of the voice of God is trying to penetrate through the things that are occupying the places in your mind He needs to reach. We can easily hear the voice of God when we are in a place of trust and complete faith in Jesus! For *in Him there is no fault, for Jesus is called the righteousness of God. So how can He not be trustworthy with your burdens, and things concerning you?*

1 Corinthians 1:30, "But of Him are ye in Christ Jesus, who of God is made unto us wisdom, and righteousness, and sanctification, and redemption.

1 John 2:1, " My little children, these things write I unto you, that ye sin not. And if any man sin, we have an advocate with the Father, Jesus Christ the righteous.

Romans 3:10-13, " As it is written, There is none righteous, no, not one: There is none that understandeth, there is no that seeketh after God. They are all gone out of the way, they are together become unprofitable; there is none that doeth good, no, not one. Their throat is an open sepulchre; with their tongues they have used deceit; the poison of asps is under their lips.

So, JESUS, the precious Son of God is He that is the Only Righteous One that has walked on the earth, and He is the Only True Righteous that *shall ever be.* It is *by Him that we are made righteous in the eyes of God.* For t*he righteousness of God is by having faith in Jesus Christ*, for there is no other way to reach the approval of God but in Christ Jesus! Those of you who believe in the Once Saved Always Saved Doctrine ye are in great error, and also are in danger of immediate hellfire if you do not reconcile yourself unto God through Jesus Christ receive the True Doctrine of God. For the word has already been done for you through the redemptive work of Jesus Christ! Amen.

With saying that, JESUS, being God should be the only One that we should trust because He righteous. I have brought before you the scriptures of God, *believe Him for He is good! Cast all thy cares upon the Lord for He careth for you(1 Peter 5:7).*

My petition unto the saints of God

I have a great petition, I ask that as your brother in the faith to pray for me. I am but a man serving our God, with that comes accusations, plots, evil devices at work against me. I ask that your prayers be from a place of sincerity, not jealous, and also love. I pray that you have consumed the pages of this book, and the teachings *from God* for He gave me the authority and the desire to write such a book. He shall receive the glory for this one, any glory that is brought to my name I will cast it down from my name and lift it up to Jesus! He is my *Rock, my Salvation, my Deliverer, my Redeemer, and the lover of my soul it is He that has kept me all this time.* Nothing that I have done has got me here, but by me putting my faith in Jesus Christ He has shifted my life into the pleasures of His Holy Will. I am not ashamed to be one of His, but I am glad to be *called chosen by God.* I thank Thee, O Heavenly Father, for your wonderful love and matchless power and excellence! You have got me here, and for that I will glorify thee until the end of my days, Amen.

Epilouge of Exaltation unto the throne of Jesus the mighty Lamb of God

God you have created all things in existence for your pleasure and by Your Own Will. I am part of your creation, and I will praise thee unto the ends of the earth, even in the heavens when I meet you. From the fruit of my lips will come forth praises unto Your throne, and unto the Lamb of God. For He has saved us from our sins O God, He that Thou hast sent. He has become the image of the invisible God, so it is He that I worship and praise! I thank Thee O Thou Mighty Son of God, for thou hast created me, and has formed me in the belly of mother's womb, and hast known me before my form was shaped. Before the foundation of the earth hast thou chosen me, and many others I pray unto Thee O Father that thou will save many through me. I want your glorification to be my legacy, I want to be known as a man that was upright before God the Savior. I am not strong on my own, Jesus, so I need Thee to help me endure what is coming after the publication of this book, I need Thee O God. Forsake me not in this time, for You know that I have been before you, forget me not Jesus.

I understand that Thou I am yours, and that you will keep me in that time O God. You are a beautiful and an excellent God! You are not a man that shall lie, neither are Thou a like a son of man that you should repent but You Are the Righteous, even Jesus. I thank Thee O God of Zion that thou art with me, and how that hast saved me from the death penalty that comes from sin. I cannot forget thy commandments, thy praises, or thy Name for they are great! I am in love with your laws and commandments! I understand that you should get all the glory, and I as your servant and son that give it unto Thee through my life. You shall be pleased with me, O Lord, for I will follow you for the rest of the days of my life. Thank You O Lord for Your anointing that has gifted me with through the gifting of the Holy Ghost, for now I have the power to be your son, and move by Your Holy Spirit, Amen. Be thou glorified in me O God, for I am Your vessel to use! Hallelujah Jesus! For you said in Your Word in that great day, *"And I, if I be lifted up from the earth, will draw all men unto Me."* So, Father, as I lifted up Your Name above my own and all others, *draw all men* unto Your Holy fold, Amen.

The Father's Response

" *I AM He that liveth, and AM He that understands all things, because I AM He that hath created ALL things in the heavens as well as the earth. I am He that hath called you, and all those who are of My fold, My People. Nothing shall separate Me from you, I will do as you ask, and I will glorify Myself in you that I all men who have an ear will hear and come. I AM He that calleth and He that knocks at the door of the readers of this book in which I've validated and approved with Mine Own Hand. I AM Him that causeth the demons to tremble, so, whatever they plan against you you will be safe from it. I will push them away from you to a place where they cannot touch you, nor shall you be able to hear their voice. For I am a God that doesn't stand by as other gods do and let their people suffer while they call on My Name, for when they call I hear them and answer. I don't hear them and sit still, but I immediately show up to the scene. I am not made of gold, nor of silver, nor of the wood of trees, nor the ground that you walk upon, the cement, nor AM I made of clay, nor was I crafted by the minds of men, but all these things that are list I, the Lord, have created for My purpose and Will as you have thus said. I hear thee always son, thou knowest that I cannot forget Thee nor will I ever attempt to do so, son. But when you call I will show up and handle the situations that shall arise from the publication of this book. For I will push you forward as they try to push you down and contain you. For I will cover thee with a hedge of protection that no devil in hell can enter, nor any witch, or any spell for I will breathe on My people for them to be cleansed from the evil that men try to attach to their names, including yours, son. Hear Me, your Lord, for I will cause you to work in the field as My minister, and ye shall reap the harvest here on the earth and in the heavens. Hear Me, those who read you too can reach the level that you will witness you shall see My son be elevated to by Me. However, if thou allowest thyself to become jealous of your brother you shall not see the harvest of thy works, but it shall be cut short because of thy unwillingness to focus on Me rather than men. I AM He that created you, do thou think that I can't elevate thee? I am the God who does not look at the work rather than the heart of the one doing the work. If you have not the love of God in you, you are as a clashing set of symbols in My ears! And if thou art, I shall cast thee from My presence unless thee repent! You are now living in a time where Christianity, the belief of My Son is being targeted and will one day called a threat to humanity according to their way of life, for they fear not Me, but willingly blaspheme My Name with their lips and dishonor Me with their bodies. I will get the glory, and all will bow and confess Me as Lord, the Savior that I AM. I AM He," saith the Lord of all lords, the God of all gods, and the King of all kings!*

Amen! To God the Father, the Son, and the Holy be the glory forever and ever, Amen!